FOREWORD BY RUSSELL BRUNSON

CHALLENGE
SECRETS

How To Turn Ice Cold Traffic Into Red Hot Buyers in 5 Days or Less

FHL 2023
Special "Linchpin" Edition

PEDRO ADAO

CHALLENGE SECRETS

How To Turn Ice Cold Traffic Into Red Hot Buyers in 5 Days or Less

Copyright © 2023 Pedro Adao. All rights reserved. No part of this publication may be reproduced, distributed, or transmitted in any form or by any means, including photocopying, recording, or other electronic or mechanical methods, without the prior written permission of the copyright holder, except in the case of brief quotations embodied in critical reviews and certain other noncommercial uses permitted by law.

For permission requests, speaking inquiries, podcast interviews, and bulk order purchase options, visit: 828support.com

PedroAdao.com

Book Design by Transcendent Publishing
TranscendentPublishing.com

Author's photos (front and back cover) by Christina Cho Serrano
Front cover design by The Lovely Lyss
Proofreading by Mary Rembert

ISBN: 979-8-9890682-2-7

Disclaimer: The author makes no guarantees concerning the level of success you may experience by following any information or methods contained in this book. The testimonials and examples provided in this book show exceptional results, which may not apply to the average reader. Thus the publisher nor the author assumes any liability for any losses that may be sustained by the use of information or methods described in this book, and any such liability is expressly disclaimed. The use of this book implies your acceptance of this disclaimer.

Printed in the United States of America.

Everything you want in your life and business is on the other side of you crushing it with challenges.

—Pedro Adao

ATTENTION

This special *Linchpin Edition* is an abbreviated version of the full *Challenge Secrets* book, coming soon! To get on the waiting list to be notified when the full version launches, go to:

www.ChallengeSecrets.com/book

NOTE: This galley copy is not permitted for resale or distribution.

CONTENTS

Warning vii

Foreword by Russell Brunson ix

What If Russell Is Right? xiii

The Case for Challenges 1

    Challenge Secret #1 7

    Challenge Secret #2 19

    Challenge Secret #3 23

Section One: Challenge Design 25

    Challenge Secret #4 29

    Challenge Secret #5 33

    Challenge Secret #6 39

    Challenge Secret #7 49

    Challenge Secret #8 61

Section Two: How To Run a Live Challenge 63

    Challenge Secret #9 67

    Challenge Secret #10 79

    Challenge Secret #11 85

    Challenge Secret #12 89

    Challenge Secret #13 93

Section Three: Promoting Your Challenge 95

    Challenge Secret #14 97

    Challenge Secret #15 105

Free Gift 109
Can I Challenge You? 111
About the Author 117

WARNING

The most influential online marketers today credit me as the innovative force behind one of today's most popular and effective marketing tools: challenges.

At the time of this writing, I have run over 75 profitable live challenges in the past five years. I am the creator of the best and most consumed training on challenges in the world.

And now, for the first time ever, I'm distilling my method into a direct, to-the-point book that will teach you how you can use challenges to radically multiply your marketing efforts.

In this book I'm going to teach you…

- What a challenge is

- What a challenge isn't

- How and why challenges are so effective

- How to come up with creative challenge ideas

- What to teach each day of your challenge and

Ultimately, how to get as many of your challenge participants as possible to purchase your offer.

But first, a warning…

After using challenges exclusively for over five years to generate close to $50 Million in revenue for my own business; after teaching challenges to tens of thousands of students for the past three years; after consulting on dozens of challenges with some of the most well-known entrepreneurs on the planet; I have to make one thing perfectly clear.

Your Challenge Will Flop If...

Not all challenges are created equal. Some challenges make five figures, some six, seven, and even multiple millions of dollars. But most challenges completely flop—or at least fail to produce the results the entrepreneur was hoping for.

What separates challenges that flop from challenges that crush it?

To answer that question and help you get the most out of this book, I made you a free training you should watch right now at ChallengeSecrets.com/Start before you read any further.

Crushing it With Challenges is Step 3 of my 3-Step Framework. Which means, if you skip steps 1 and 2, your challenge will flop.

So go now to **ChallengeSecrets.com/Start** for a free short training on steps 1 and 2 so you can get the most out of this book and avoid a failed challenge.

FOREWORD
Russell Brunson

Nearly a decade ago, I launched a software company called ClickFunnels. Around the same time, I released my very first book, *Dotcom Secrets*. It was the first book ever written that taught people about funnels, funnel structure, funnel design, and how to use funnels to substantially grow their businesses. In the first edition of that book, I shared various types of funnels, but there is one that wasn't listed in that first edition: the challenge funnel. At that time, nobody was really doing challenges.

A few years later, when I updated the book for a second edition, I added a chapter on paid challenge funnels. The reason I added this chapter is that we had just launched the One Funnel Away Challenge. Today, we've had over 120,000 people invest $100 to go through that challenge. This challenge was a game-changer for our business. It took us from having around 50,000 active monthly members to over 100,000.

Shortly after the release of the second edition of *Dotcom Secrets*, someone named Pedro Adao joined my Inner Circle. When Pedro first went up on stage, he told us how God had "tricked" him into starting his own business. In order to do this, Pedro started doing free challenges. At that point in time, there was hardly anyone doing free online challenges. I watched Pedro take this concept and start innovating, developing, and growing it into one of the most profitable types of funnels in the world. Thanks in large part to Pedro's innovation, it became one of our favorite funnels to use. We use it almost every month now!

So when Pedro told me he wanted to write this book dedicated to the challenge funnel, with his own twist on how they work, which he developed over the last five years, I was super excited. In today's market, it's hard to find true innovators of how businesses are done online. Pedro is one of those people.

Today, when I open my Facebook feed, I see dozens of people launching challenges every single week. You might wonder if that means that challenges are overdone. Without a doubt in my mind, I can tell you the answer is NO. They work better now than ever, especially if you follow the principles Pedro lays out in this book.

Once you learn how to figure out exactly who your dream customer is, and how to design a challenge that specifically speaks to them, you have the key to get them to step into your world and become a part of your movement. This book lays out the path to acquiring new customers, indoctrinating them, and getting them to fall in love with you, not just long enough for them to just buy your products and services, but to get them to become a committed, die-hard fan. They become a lifetime customer and a champion for your cause. Challenges give you the ability to bond with your customers in a way that no other funnel type does.

Reading through this book, even with the hindsight of having launched over a dozen challenges in about five or six different companies (often with Pedro's expert guidance), I still discovered and learned so many things. If you have already been using challenge funnels, this book is full of tips and tricks that will increase your traffic and conversion. And if you haven't, this is the definite blueprint to launching your first one. Pedro is the pioneer who first developed and innovated this groundbreaking strategy. There's no one better out there to teach you how to turn a small following into a full-fledged, world-changing movement. Prepare to enter a world where challenges are not just business tools, they are truly transformative experiences.

–**Russell Brunson**

WHAT IF RUSSELL IS RIGHT?

December 13, 2022 – Boise, Idaho

It was a cold, snowy Wednesday in Boise, Idaho. I was at Russell Brunson's downtown Boise penthouse, otherwise known as the Snow Globe, for a meeting of his Atlas Inner Circle for Life Mastermind.

I really didn't feel like going. I was just getting over being sick and I was very preoccupied with my biggest challenge of the year—the 31 Day Wisdom Challenge—that was coming up. On top of that, I hate cold weather and knew it was going to be freezing in Boise.

But for some reason, I had a nagging feeling that I was really supposed to be there, so off I went to Boise.

It was the last day of meetings. I had made a couple of notes for ideas that came to me over the previous three days, but frankly, I didn't feel the trip was worth it.

Then, during lunch on our very last day, I got a gift that changed everything. Right before lunch, one of the presenters asked the group for feedback. While Russell answered their question, he referred to the "Linchpin" several times.

"What's a Linchpin?" I thought. I leaned over to Russell. "Bro, I'm pretty sure none of us here know what the heck a Linchpin is."

In classic Russell fashion, he said, "What do you mean? Are you serious?" We were, after all, in his highest-level mastermind, exclusive to entrepreneurs making more than $10 million in annual revenue. "I taught this at Funnel Hacking Live. What do you mean you don't know what this is?" But as I looked around the room, all I saw were blank faces. It was clear no one knew what the Linchpin was.

After asking the group himself, Russell realized I was right. So, Russell decided to break down the Linchpin for us during our lunch break.

I'd like to say the heavens parted, and I fully grasped the power of the Linchpin while Russell explained it, but that's not what happened. I for sure got a better understanding of it, but I wouldn't actually get it till later.

WHAT IF RUSSELL IS RIGHT?

The Linchpin Framework

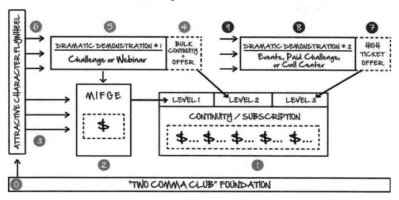

During Russell's lunchtime presentation of the Linchpin, he again quoted one of his mentors, David Frey: **"If you don't have continuity, you don't have a real business."** The Linchpin is all about continuity. As you can see from the graphic, all roads, or in this case, all the arrows point to the continuity or recurring revenue subscription program.

On the flight home later that day, I thought it would be smart to review my notes, and there it was in my notebook. **"If you don't have continuity, you don't have a real business."** I've heard Russell say this for the past five years, and it pretty much went in one ear and out the other because I was having so much success. God tricked me into running my first free challenge in May of 2018, and just my 2nd full year online, I had my first 8-figure year in 2020.

Let me tell you about my first challenge.

At the time, I was a financial professional running a very successful retirement planning business. I had recently just had my first ever million-dollar year. I had big plans to expand my financial business nationally but hit some unexpected bumps in the road. "Coincidentally," around that time I was having a passionate conversation with a friend after church where I was complaining about something that really bothered me. And after letting me finish my epic rant, he asked me a question that changed my life, "So what are you going to do about it?"

"Me, what am I supposed to do about this?" I asked. "I'm just a financial planner living in Vacaville, California. I'm not famous; nobody knows who I am. I don't have a platform or any social media following. What could I possibly do to help with this?"

He said, "Why don't you do a class? Teach people what you had to learn the hard way. Share what you have learned on your journey to becoming a 7-Figure Kingdom Entrepreneur."

So, on the drive home from church, my wife and I talked, and we agreed to do a class. But instead of hosting a class at the church as my friend suggested, we decided to do it online.

So I built a very simple and very ugly 3-page funnel and spent approximately $3,000 in paid ads, promoting it to complete strangers, not having any idea if anybody would care. I had about 300 people participate in the challenge, with about 100 of them really engaged. I let them know that I was going to do two to three live trainings a week during the month of June.

What surprised me is that by week two, people in the challenge started to DM me with incredibly positive comments about how much they loved the training.

I was getting messages from so many people saying things like, "You're my guy. I've been waiting so long for something like this!" "Whatever you're selling, I'm buying. Shoot me the link. I want to sign up!"

I really wasn't expecting this overwhelming response. I responded to these messages: "Thanks for the feedback. So glad you're getting so much value from my training, but I don't have a link. I don't have anything to sell you."

"What do you mean you have nothing to sell me? Stop playing around and just send me the link. There's no way you're doing all this work and have nothing to sell us."

But the truth is, I didn't have anything to sell them. God really did trick me into doing this through the dare of a friend, and I really didn't have any plans of launching a new business.

But the people in my challenge were relentless as the weeks went on and as we got closer to the end of the challenge. More and more people kept messaging me and wouldn't leave me alone. They insisted that I come up with something to sell them so we could continue what we started in this challenge.

So, after praying about this with my wife Suzette, we decided to launch the 100X Academy as a 12-month training program. We had about 30 people jump into my newly formed coaching program for $997 for a year. Suddenly, I had committed to teaching these 30 people for the next 12 months, so I figured I should go get more students, help more people, and make some more money to make all this worth my time.

So I ran another free challenge in July. And again, complete strangers, people who had no idea who I was, were enthusiastic about joining my paid coaching program after spending five days with me.

Five years later, I've never stopped running challenges; I was able to become the #1 go-to expert / brand in two different niches. I have launched international movement-based businesses, trained hundreds of thousands of people in my free challenges, enrolled thousands of complete strangers directly into my training programs, put on the biggest events in my niche, and have earned tens of millions of dollars without ever having a "membership" or recurring revenue.

Considering how well I was doing, why take Russell's advice? Surely the Linchpin idea didn't apply to me because I had a real business—even without continuity. But for some reason, on the flight home from this mastermind, I asked myself a question that, without exaggeration, has shifted how I think about my business forever.

What if Russell is right?

What if I don't have a real business?

So on the short flight home from Boise to California, I played a game with myself. I chose to "temporarily" believe that I didn't have a real business because I didn't have any recurring revenue.

Therefore, the obvious first question was: how and where does a membership or continuity offer **best fit** into my business?

When you ask the right question, it's incredible how fast the right answer can appear. Literally, as soon as I was done asking myself the question of "where a membership program best fits into my business," I immediately got the answer.

And within approximately 30 days of that cold and snowy December mastermind meeting that I almost didn't go to, I launched my first-ever monthly membership offer. Toward the end of my 31-Day Wisdom Challenge that I do every January, I launched a brand-new membership program called Kingdom Seekers.

Over the next week, I had over 4,000 people sign up for a $31 dollar/month membership to get daily content, coaching, and community from me and my team.

What happened next is hard to explain. It's like in an instant it all clicked, and everything I thought was right and what I was doing to grow my business got flipped completely upside down. It's really hard to explain just how massive of a paradigm shift this was for me.

I realized Russell was right.

While I've been wildly successful running challenges and 3-day virtual and in-person events for the last five years, having generated over $40 million in sales from 2020 - 2023, none of that revenue came in the form of recurring subscription income.

Approximately one-third of many of my customers chose to join my programs by paying in full, while the other two-thirds joined on a payment plan. I used to think that recurring revenue and payment plans were the same since both create a form of monthly cash flow. However, payment plans are very different than a true recurring subscription revenue. Payment plans eventually end, while a subscription is never paid up. It only stops if the customer chooses to cancel.

At the time of writing this book, it's been eight months since I've officially had a monthly subscription membership. I've also had the opportunity to be at two more mastermind events with Russell, where he further explained the Linchpin.

While this might be a tough pill to swallow, if you don't have continuity, you probably don't have a real business. Or at least not a predictable business that somebody would ever be willing to write you a big check for one day. For me, it has been an interesting shift and a detox of sorts as I've become more focused on creating additional recurring revenue, even sometimes at the expense of immediate upfront cash.

Don't get me wrong, I'm still running live challenges to acquire new customers and to bring immediate upfront lump sums of cash into the business. The difference is I'm now doing that while simultaneously looking to grow my recurring revenue at the same time.

That's why the Linchpin is such a powerful framework and truly is the secret behind how Russell grew ClickFunnels to over $100M a year in revenue. I've heard him say on multiple occasions that every company he owns is now running the Linchpin as the sole customer acquisition plan.

This, plus the fact that the Linchpin was going to be a major focus of FHL 2023, is why I decided to create this special *Challenge Secrets - Linchpin Edition*.

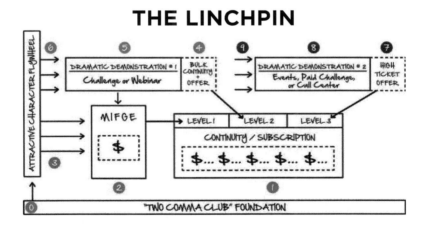

What I've Learned from The Linchpin

When properly implemented, the Linchpin will allow you to experience what could possibly be the best possible business outcome you could ever hope for: How to get paid now to then also get paid again month after month—**at the same time.**

You may want to read that again. With a well-designed Linchpin, you get to make money now while increasing your monthly cash flow all at the same time. As far as business goes, I'm pretty sure there is literally nothing better than that.

There is one and only one reason your business will fail…and that's if you run out of money. While there could be many reasons a business runs out of money, there's only one reason why a business fails, goes bankrupt, and ultimately ends up closing shop. It's because the business owner ran out of money.

IMPORTANT QUESTION

If there was a way to all but guarantee your business would never fail, and that you could make money today while creating increasing monthly recurring revenue all at the same time, how serious would you be about putting that to work in your business?

Now that you hopefully see the power of implementing the Linchpin in your business, why continue reading *Challenge Secrets?*

What if I told you that out of the nine elements of the Linchpin framework, one is more important than all the rest? What if I told you there's a Linchpin to the Linchpin?

The most important element of the Linchpin framework is element #5 – The Challenge.

So before you go run off to learn about the Linchpin, you would do yourself a huge favor by finishing this book and learning these Challenge Secrets first.

The reason I was able to launch a 7-figure subscription membership the very first time I tried is because I sold it during one of my most successful challenges.

If you look at every single one of Russell's businesses that is using the Linchpin right now, every one of them is using a live or evergreen Challenge. The great majority of the traffic for each business is being driven directly to the challenge or to other front-end funnels that end up pushing people into the challenge.

This book in your hands has my Challenge Secrets. If you can master these Challenge Secrets you will be well on your way to being able to successfully implement the Linchpin.

My hope and prayer for you is that my Challenge Secrets will bring you unimaginable joy, fulfillment, and financial blessings, just as they have for me.

Your Friend,

Pedro "The Challenge Guy" Adao

THE CASE FOR CHALLENGES

September 23, 2021 - Orlando Florida

I had just finished coming off stage at Funnel Hacking Live—basically the Super Bowl of online marketing—to a crowd of over 4,000 people known as Funnel Hackers. My talk was all about my challenge marketing system that I'd been teaching to thousands of entrepreneurs all around the world. FHL was my dream stage. Ever since Russell asked me to speak at this event, I'd been praying it'd go well.

I remember the day Russell called me on FaceTime to ask me to speak at FHL. I'm pretty sure I said yes before he was even finished asking me. Months later, the day finally came, and I got to take the stage on Day 3 of FHL 2021. To say I was nervous would be an understatement. I prepared more for this presentation than anything I had ever done before; this truly was my dream stage, and I was still ridiculously nervous.

I remember being backstage, standing behind the massive LED wall that opens up right before they announce your name, and I literally couldn't feel my legs. This made me especially nervous because I was walking out to "Turn Down For What" by Lil Jon, and I was planning on getting the crowd hyped by jumping up and down with event MC Devon Brown.

Fortunately, the talk went incredibly well. Frankly, better than I could have dreamed or imagined. I was so relieved that on the biggest stage of my life, I was able to represent Russell well, represent myself well, and most importantly, show the thousands of Funnel Hackers in attendance how they can have everything they want in their life and business by learning how to Crush It with Challenges.

As I walked back to my seat amid all the hustle and bustle in the hallway of the conference center, I heard a woman with a thick Texas accent yelling, "Pedro…Pedro…I need to talk to you!" When I looked back, I realized it was one of my students, Tresa.

I had only met Tresa once before when she came to a small event I held in January of 2020 at Country Music Legend Reba McEntire's former mansion in Nashville. This was a three-day workshop-style event where, for the first time ever, I taught every aspect of my new challenge marketing system in front of a small group of students.

I'm terrible with names but rarely forget a face, so I immediately remembered Tresa. She then proceeded to start thanking me and let me know that since she last saw me, she had run *seven challenges in a row, each bringing in over $1 million in sales* for her real estate investing program.

I remember hearing this and starting to laugh. Thinking I must have misheard her, I asked, "What did you say?" and she told me the same thing again, this time a little slower, that she and her team had successfully run seven challenges in a row, each generating over $1 million in sales.

I had to know more. We grabbed a seat off to the side, and she told me how she did it. She said that when she first came back from the event, she didn't do anything—she threw her notebook in a closet in her office and forgot about it. Her business was doing just fine. She didn't see a need to fix what wasn't broken.

But then, a month or so later, the world shut down during the pandemic—and so did Tresa's ability to grow her business. For years, Tresa and her sons Justin and Kelton had built their business by doing local events at hotels throughout the Dallas area, and now all her scheduled events that had already been promoted and paid for got canceled.

She recalled how, during a meeting with her team, she went and pulled her notebook full of notes from my event out of her closet and slid the notebook across the table to her sons. "I know the way forward," she said. "It's called a challenge, and everything you need to know is in this notebook, so figure it out," and she left the room.

And figure it out they did. Not only did my challenge marketing system save her business from failure during the pandemic, but it's continued to be her one and only marketing strategy that has propelled her company to the top as the biggest women's real estate investor network in America and maybe the world.

Now, Tresa and I are part of the same Mastermind. Last I saw her, she had shared that her company had just finished 2022 with $37 million in sales—all on the back of the challenge model Tresa learned at my first-ever challenge training.

You may be thinking that Tresa is an exception. And while she's exceptional, she's not the first to tell me how challenges transformed their business. My challenge model is responsible for helping thousands of entrepreneurs not only save their existing businesses during the pandemic but also helping thousands more launch, grow, and scale their businesses in almost every niche imaginable.

It was my Challenge Secrets that helped Tony Robbins continue to grow his businesses when COVID shut down all his in-person stadium events all over the world. Tony, with the help of his partner Dean Graziosi and my good friends Bari and Blue of Sage, quickly pivoted to delivering his life-changing events virtually. And it is many of my Challenge Secrets covered in this book that they've used to sell hundreds of thousands of tickets to his live virtual and now in-person events since 2020.

You might be thinking that challenges are only for big-time entrepreneurs like Tresa and Tony Robbins. But what if I told you that my Challenge Secrets have helped countless early-stage entrepreneurs, people who had previously never had success online, finally break through?

I hear all the time from people around the world who are struggling to make this online thing work. They were doing all the things—posting free content every day, podcasting, blogging, offering free lead magnets, and running webinars—with little to no results. Until they finally tried a challenge.

In this book, I will reveal some of the most important Challenge Secrets, but before we dive in, let's make sure you understand what a challenge is and why they're so effective.

What Is a Challenge, And Why Do They Work?

A challenge is, by far, the most effective and underutilized marketing strategy currently available to entrepreneurs. A challenge is a time-bound offering to an entrepreneur's audience that invites them to take immediate action, offers accountability and training, and guides them toward a specific, highly desired result. Entrepreneurs who run successful challenges create:

- **Urgency**: making their challenge available for only a limited period of time—usually 5 to 10 days.

- **Massive Action**: everyone in the challenge agrees to be pushed and to take action.

- **Momentum**: the live daily trainings and assignments help participants overcome obstacles and put them in momentum in the direction of the desired outcome.

Challenges are marketing made simple. They allow you to deliver real value and results to your challenge participants in advance. And now that they know, like, and trust you, your challenge participants are much more likely to want to take the next step with you into your paid programs.

Which brings me to Challenge Secret #1. I think the reason so many entrepreneurs struggle to have success with their online marketing is because they are trying to learn too many things at the same time—from social media growth and podcasting to email lists and lead magnets. Most are highly distracted, making it impossible to ever get any real momentum or get good at anything.

Maybe this story sounds all too familiar. Maybe you too have tried all the things and you're still nowhere closer to the business and income you want. Then here is Challenge Secret #1 to the rescue.

CHALLENGE SECRET #1
You're Just One *Challenge* Funnel Away

Russell Brunson is famous for saying you're just one funnel away. But when we were together in Mexico at the Mastermind In Paradise, we took advantage of being together to shoot some ads for the Challenge Secrets. And it was during the shooting of those ads that I had the opportunity to "pin" Russell down and make him answer a question I've wanted him to answer for years.

"Russell, I know you're the Funnel guy and that you love all the funnels. But if you could only use one funnel...one and only one funnel to grow ClickFunnels, which funnel would it be?"

"Oh man, Pedro, I hate to admit this...but the truth is if I could only use one and only one funnel to build my businesses, it would be a Challenge."

Therefore, in the next few pages, I am going to prove to you what Russell and I already know, that a well-designed challenge funnel is the one and only funnel you need to launch, grow, and scale your entire business.

This secret has been hiding in plain sight for the past few years, but I'm going to take you behind the curtain and share something with you that the smartest marketers in our industry already know. When Dean Graziosi and Tony Robbins launched their brand-new mastermind program, they did it with a challenge. When Russell Brunson launched the brand new version of ClickFunnels, he did it with a challenge. When Eric and Marina Worre wanted to sell tens of thousands of tickets to their GoPro event, they ran a challenge.

So the question you should be asking yourself is this...

If the smartest marketers in the business are leveraging challenges, why aren't you?

Maybe, just maybe, they know something you don't. They do. I shared my Challenge Secrets with them, and now I'm going to share them with you.

So let me explain Challenge Secret #1...

You're just one challenge funnel away.

I first heard about the concept of the value ladder from Russell Brunson.

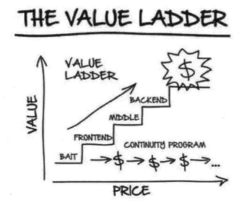

As you can see from the image, the lower end of the value ladder starts with something free, sometimes referred to as bait or a lead magnet. At the top of the ladder is your most expensive, highest-value, highest-ticket offer.

The value ladder is so much more powerful than most people realize. A well-designed value ladder is effectively your business and marketing plan, all in one, and on one page. It doesn't get any simpler than that. From a business plan perspective, your value ladder makes it clear what business you're in. Whatever is on that value ladder is what you are in the business of selling and doing at a profit.

From a marketing perspective, your value ladder can also be a one-page marketing plan, making it clear that the primary goal of your marketing process is to get people to request your free offering and then as quickly and profitably as possible to get them to want to give you money for your highest-value, highest price offering.

I hope you caught that. From my experience, the simplest concepts are the most powerful and also the easiest to miss. The goal of an effective marketing plan is the following.

1. Get complete strangers to gladly give you their name, email, and phone number for something you're offering for free.

2. After consuming your free thing, sell them on one of your paid offers.

3. And as quickly as possible, ascend them to your premium high-ticket programs.

Yes, it really is this simple. So now that you understand the goal of an effective marketing plan, let me show you how a well-designed challenge allows you to achieve all these goals at the same time.

There are two main types of challenges: free challenges and paid challenges. Both are awesome and super effective. Let me show you how a well-designed free challenge allows you to do what no other funnel can do: climb the entire value ladder in one step.

Free Bait / Lead Magnet

The primary goal of a free lead magnet is to build your email list. Once someone has provided their name, email, and maybe even their phone number, you can now continue to email them in hopes of building a relationship and having them eventually buy one of your paid offerings.

I believe the most valuable free lead magnet you could offer your prospective customer is a well-designed, free five-day challenge. Most lead magnets kind of suck, and a well-designed free five-day challenge is way better than any other option. How could a checklist, a report, or a short free training ever be as valuable as a five-day challenge where you deliver an hour of your best training five days in a row?

Most of my students come to me with a typical, failing lead magnet funnel—usually driven by PDFs and checklists. But once they learned my Challenge Secrets and started running free, five-day challenges, they were finally able to start building an email list. Whereas common lead magnets like PDFs feel like homework, challenges deliver real, instant value alongside the accountability to reach your goal.

Key Point: A free challenge is the *best* lead magnet.

Low-Ticket / Tripwire Offer

Once you've earned a name, email, and phone number, the next step is to convert your lead to a paying customer as soon as possible.

Usually, that means offering a low-priced product. The old way of doing this was by emailing your new lead every day and asking them to buy a low-ticket offer. Depending on your niche, this could be something priced as low as $7 and maybe as much as $97.

In the early days of online marketing, this worked pretty well when email open rates were much higher, and there just weren't as many people taking advantage of online marketing. But today, email open rates are significantly lower because this strategy is so overused. In our new marketing landscape, the best way to make your first sale to someone new on your email list is to invite them to upgrade and become a VIP in your challenge.

We do this right in the Free Challenge Funnel, which makes it super easy for you and your new customer. Below is a doodle of what the funnel looks like. The first page of the Free Challenge Funnel is an Opt-In page. This is the page where you share with them all the info about your upcoming challenge, and they say yes to wanting to be a part of it by giving you their name, email, and phone number.

Then, once they click the submit button, the next page of the challenge funnel is going to invite them to be a VIP in your challenge. Typically, a VIP upgrade is priced around $37 - $97 and comes with some special perks available only to VIPs.

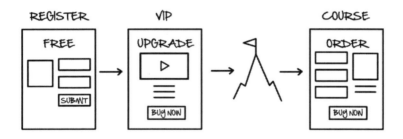

I have seen so many of my students generate hundreds and even thousands of brand-new leads and customers this way, even when nothing they had tried before worked.

The Middle or Core Offer

Once you've made that initial sale, your lead is now a buyer. I don't want you to underestimate the importance of getting someone to give you $7, $37, or $97. A list of buyers will be worth substantially more to your business than just a list of emails because someone who has purchased something from you, even if it's relatively inexpensive, is much more likely to buy something from you again, and again, and again. And that next purchase is hopefully something more expensive, bringing us to the next step in the value ladder.

In the information/coaching space, this next purchase is usually a course or group coaching program priced as low as $295 and as much as $2,995. The old way of doing this was with lengthy sales letters, video sales letters, or webinars. And while in some cases, there are entrepreneurs that are still able to profitably grow their business with these old-school methods, it is by far the exception. Without a doubt, the #1 way to sell a course or group coaching program today is with a challenge.

After you have spent five days helping the people you want to serve get a real result they want to achieve, naturally, a percentage of them are going to want more. More coaching, more training. They are going to want to continue and stay in the progress and momentum you helped create for them in their challenge.

This is why the biggest course launches each and every year are now done using my 5-Day Challenge Framework. Dean Graziosi and Tony Robbins of MasterMind.com, Grant Cardone's 10X, and Russell Brunson's ClickFunnels are all companies doing over $100 Million a year in revenue that use my 5-Day Challenge Funnel when wanting to sell the most amount of courses in the least amount of time. I could also spend all day making a list of 8-figure entrepreneurs like myself as well as 7-figure and multi-seven-figure entrepreneurs who use challenges as their primary, if not only, marketing strategy.

I worked with Roland Frasier back in 2020 and helped him create his 5-Day Epic Challenge. Last time I checked in with Roland, he had run essentially that same challenge over 20 times and generated well over $10 Million in sales just from that one challenge.

The High-Ticket Offer

You may be thinking, "Pedro, that's great and all, but how can I use challenges to sell my most premium, highest-priced stuff?" I'm so glad you asked that question because it seems like as the online information and coaching industry matures, more and more people are selling as well as purchasing high-ticket offers. And while I and many of my peers and students have been able to profitably sell our lower-priced courses (typically $997 - $1,997) on the back end of our challenge, the bulk of the profit generated in an information/coaching business comes from the high-ticket offer.

So let's finish off this value ladder conversation by having me show you the two primary ways you can generate sales of your high-ticket program with challenges.

1. **At the end of your challenge, instead of pointing people to a sales page to buy a course, you can send them to an application / book-a-call page.** This page would require them to provide you with key information about themselves and have them schedule a call with you or a salesperson on your team. On that call, it is so much simpler and easier to get them to convert into a high-ticket buyer because you can use your offering to address their individual pain points. If you are nervous that you will get too many people booking calls, you can

charge a deposit and or share the price of the program before giving them the opportunity to book a call.

2. You can host a live event after the challenge. One thing I have done very successfully with the help of my good friend and industry-leading expert Bari Baumgardner of Sage, is to host three-day virtual events for my customers. What's nice about this three-day event that is different than my 5-Day Challenge is that it is three immersive days. These are generally six- to ten-hour days, three days in a row, so it allows you to go really deep and cover a lot of ground. While there is a ton of value and learning that happens in these three-day events—what Bari calls her 3-Day PAG—the main goal is to get people in attendance to want to take part in your high-ticket offer. So if the idea of doing sales calls or hiring and managing a sales team doesn't sound like much fun, you can do this. When you run your challenge, you can bundle in a free ticket to your three-day event as a bonus, or you can even sell a ticket to your three-day event as the offer on the back of your challenge.

Secret #1 is the most important of all the Challenge Secrets. A well-designed Challenge is the one and only marketing strategy and funnel you need because it's the only marketing strategy and funnel that allows you to achieve every objective of the entire value ladder at the same time. This has been one of the most important secrets to my success with both of my companies. I was able to hit over $10M in sales in just my second year online, and there is no way that would have been possible without my challenge model.

The old way of ascending the value ladder required a different funnel for each step...

- A lead-magnet funnel to build your email list

- A low-ticket tripwire funnel to make your first sale

- A webinar funnel to sell your core offer and…

- A high-ticket application funnel to sell your most exclusive and expensive programs.

The old way required you to build not just four different funnels—but four funnels that actually worked! If you've been around the game of online marketing for a while, you are very aware that getting one funnel to work takes a lot of work and maybe a little luck. Imagine how much more difficult it is to get four funnels to work! This is why so many people struggle with online marketing by doing it the old way.

If you could use one and only one funnel to launch, grow, and scale your business, it should be a challenge funnel. That's why I believe this is the first or next funnel and marketing strategy you should implement in your business right now.

CHALLENGE SECRET #1

The new way of online marketing is using my Challenge Secrets so you can achieve with one funnel in five days what used to take four weeks, months, and possibly years to achieve.

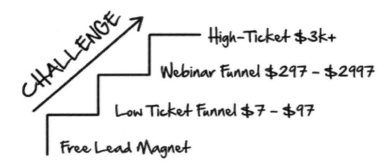

CHALLENGE SECRET #2
The Fast Track to Trust

Trust is the basis of all human relationships.

In *The Speed of Trust*, Stephen R. Covey describes trust as the act of building credibility. He bases trust on two factors: character and competency. Character is based on integrity and intention. Competency is based on capabilities and results.

In fact, the success of your business is determined by the time it takes for a complete stranger to become aware of you and your business, what you do for them, and then how long it takes for them to trust you and your ability to actually help them enough for them to give you some money.

Competency + Character = Trust

After running over 75 profitable live challenges, I can tell you nothing will help you build trust faster with people who have no idea who you are than a 5-day challenge.

Let's first discuss competency. If you are good at what you do—if you know how to get people results—nothing allows you to prove it better than with a five-day challenge. When you deliver an hour or so of your best content—live power-packed training daily for five days a row—you demonstrate your competency and expertise like no other marketing strategy.

A high-value, live interaction conveys a level of confidence that pre-recorded, heavily produced videos can't. Sure, pre-recorded content works well on social media and maybe even in your course, but when people are building trust, they want to see the real you—no filter.

Now let's address the character component of Covey's formula. Covey teaches that character is built on integrity and intention. Again, by designing and delivering an awesome 5-Day Challenge experience, your prospective customers will see what your true intentions are. "What are my true intentions, Pedro?" Well, here is what I think your intentions should be when running my challenge system:

1. To show up and serve people by delivering some of your absolute best training and helping them get the promised outcome of the challenge.

2. To grow your business and make money by inviting people who have enjoyed your challenge into your next step, which is usually to have them buy your course, coaching program, or ticket to a live event.

CHALLENGE SECRET #2

There is nothing wrong with wanting to grow your business and make money. I have found that letting people in your challenge know that these are your two primary intentions for your time together over these next five days is very effective for building trust very quickly.

When it comes to demonstrating your integrity, this happens when you show up consistently on time for those five days and deliver in your challenge what you said you were going to deliver.

> **Challenges are now and always will be incredibly effective for launching, growing, and scaling any business anywhere because they're built on principles that will never change.**

In a well-designed 5-day challenge, you get to show people just how much you care about them and the problem you are helping them to solve.

1. Just how much you **know (competency)** about the topic/situation you are helping them solve.

2. They get to **know you** and **like you** over the five days as you show up as your authentic real self.

The power of this challenge model is that it is completely in alignment with how people naturally relate and build trust with each other.

"But Pedro, what if they don't like me?" Some people won't like you, and that's totally OK. It's actually a good thing! If everyone likes you, there's a good chance you're not showing enough of your personality and values. One of the best things about challenges is that they prevent the people who shouldn't buy from you—the people who would drive you and your team crazy and probably still end up asking for a refund—from buying from you. They will probably quit the challenge before you make the invitation into your next step.

CHALLENGE SECRET #3
Anyone, Anytime, Anywhere

It's very common for a marketing strategy to work well for a more advanced entrepreneur but be difficult for a beginner. Take webinars, for example. While I wouldn't go as far as to say that webinars are dead, it seems to me that the only people having success with webinars today are very established entrepreneurs with serious amounts of social proof and testimonials as well as established brand recognition.

It's become increasingly difficult, if not downright impossible, for an entry-level entrepreneur trying to break into the market to be able to get a complete stranger to invest thousands of dollars or more with them after just a 90-minute webinar. I've heard so many stories of entrepreneurs telling me how they have spent months and even years trying to get a webinar to convert and never got there. And yet, when they applied my Challenge Secrets, they were finally able to have success launching and growing their online business.

This was the case for my students Stephen and Chelsea. They initially had some success selling their Amazon training on a webinar to people who knew them. They did around $60,000 in sales and thought they were headed to internet riches. However, once they started running ads to a cold audience, they quickly realized the webinar that worked so well with people who knew them failed miserably with a cold audience. After coming into one of my programs, they jumped on a 1:1 consulting call with me and shared their struggle. It was in that meeting that I made two very important recommendations.

One of them was to stop running the webinar and start running challenges. We then spent the rest of our time on the call mapping out a challenge.

While challenges have proven to be so much easier for beginners than webinars, unbeknownst to me, even "big name" well-established entrepreneurs were secretly having trouble profitably running cold traffic to their webinars in 2019 and 2020. That is why when I burst onto the scene with my challenge model in 2020, many of the most well-known marketers all reached out to me privately to see if I would help them run a challenge for their business.

Russell Brunson launched ClickFunnels in 2014 and relied on affiliates and the "perfect webinar" to grow it to the #1 Funnel Building Marketing Software with over 60,000 monthly subscribers. However, once they hit that number of users, they hit a ceiling. They were able to keep adding new customers by running ads to their webinar, but it was only adding enough customers to replace the ones that were canceling or pausing their membership. I recall hearing Russell say they were stuck at this level for over a year until they launched a challenge. The One Funnel Away Challenge allowed them to break past the 60,000 ClickFunnels user ceiling and take their active users to over 100,000.

This is why, of all the possible funnels Russell could have picked to be at the core of the Linchpin, a Challenge is at the center of them all.

SECTION ONE
CHALLENGE DESIGN
SECRETS

Not all challenges are equal. The success of a challenge depends on several factors, but mostly it's because of how it's designed. A challenge can do things for you and your business that no other marketing strategy can accomplish—but only if you do it right.

A well-designed challenge can produce incredible results. A poorly designed challenge can lead to unnecessary frustration that will cost you time and money. However, once you learn and apply the secrets of design, you will look like a pro, even if it's your very first challenge.

One reason challenges are so effective is because they force people to focus on one outcome. Focus is a universal problem today, and I guarantee your audience is struggling with it. ***Well-designed challenges optimize for focus.*** The goal is to get your audience focused on one goal for a limited period of time.

There are three reasons why I believe you should absolutely be using a challenge to either launch or grow your business right away.

1. Learn – You will learn more about yourself, as well as your prospective and existing customers, by running a challenge.

2. Proof – There is no better way to gather tons of social proof regarding the quality of what you do than by running a challenge.

3. Earn – You want to earn money by selling your offer at the end of the challenge to the people who are interested in going further with you.

While what I'm about to cover here in Challenge Secret #4 can be applied to any of the three desired outcomes above, it will be of most help when you want to EARN money by inviting people into your offer at the end of the challenge.

This brings me to Challenge Secret #4: **The Fool Proof Offer.**

CHALLENGE SECRET #4
Make a "Foolproof" Offer

foolproof adjective

fool·proof ˈfül-ˌprüf
Synonyms of *foolproof* >

: so simple, plain, or reliable as to leave no opportunity for error, misuse, or failure
a *foolproof* plan

I believe a foolproof offer will completely change your business. A "foolproof" offer accomplishes the two most important aspects needed for your offer to be truly successful.

1. It has to be something your prospective customer **WANTS** to buy.
2. While still delivering what they **NEED** to get the promised result/outcome.

When designing and ultimately presenting your foolproof offer to your ideal prospective customer, I believe there is one predominant thought you should focus on producing in their mind. Of all the thoughts that you may want them to think, "I'd have to be a fool not to do this" is the one that will get more people saying yes to your offer time and time again.

Like you, I've purchased all kinds of things. Both physical things like houses, cars, clothes, jewelry, and of course my fair share of books, courses, coaching, events, and masterminds. I made the most enjoyable and easiest buying decisions when I felt like I'd have to be a fool NOT to buy this.

Here's an example. In March 2023, I attended a mastermind where I ran into my friend Dr. Ben Hardy. It had been years since we had spoken, so it was fun reconnecting and catching up. During our conversation, I brought up that I was working on this book, and I had expressed concern about getting it done. As an author who's written eight books, he offered to help me process my nerves.

Toward the end of our first meeting, he asked me a question. He said, "If I was able to get you an elite badass editor, would you be willing to invest the time and money to help ensure this book gets done and that it is world-class?"

Before I even knew the price or any of the details, inside I was already saying, "Yes, yes, yes, yes. Oh my God, yes." I felt even more excited when he told me more about this editor and some of the authors she has helped. I had no idea how much this was going to cost, but I was already in. So nervously, I kept listening, waiting for Ben to tell me how much this might cost, secretly hoping it was going to be a number I could immediately say yes to.

Maybe you're someone who thinks you could never or would never immediately say yes to something, no matter how good it sounds. Maybe you have agreements in place that require you to talk to your spouse or business partner, that require you to pray about or maybe to sleep on it before making a buying decision.

Even in those cases, for some of your customers, your goal as an entrepreneur is to create a compelling offer so powerful and clear that your ideal prospect gives you an immediate yes because they know they'd be a fool not to do it.

Even if your customer says "they need to think about" before buying and ultimately gives you the yes a day or two later, I'm pretty sure they decided to purchase as soon as they heard you deliver your foolproof offer.

Once Ben finally told me what he thought it would cost me to hire this editor, it was a number I could immediately and enthusiastically say yes to. Why? Because Ben showed me the risk of NOT investing in a great editor.

The Foolproof Formula:

(Value of the Outcome to Customer X Value of Your Offer)

Divided By

(Price of Your Offer X Difficulty)

This formula is so powerful it's worth going deeper into each of the elements:

1. Pick a highly *desired* and highly *valuable* outcome your prospective customers are willing to pay for that you can deliver. The key here is what's valuable to them. Many people make the mistake of projecting their own desires, values, and budget onto their customers, which is most often a huge mistake.

2. Design and package a complete solution that can absolutely deliver on the promise of step 1. Remember, an offer is not just a product or a service. A foolproof offer includes irresistible bonuses, compelling levels of scarcity and urgency, and the perfect refund/guarantee policy that creates confidence in the mind of your customer.

3. Identify the perfect price for your foolproof offer. Low enough to create disproportionate value but not so low that it calls into question the quality or sincerity of the offer.

> **PRO TIP:** There is so much to consider when pricing your offers. The hard cost of the inputs, staff, advertising, taxes, and other factors may end up influencing a price that actually makes sense for you as the business owner. Additionally, the price of your offer also will be judged by your prospective customer.

If you are solving a very valuable problem and the price of your offer is "too low," it can backfire as your most successful and serious potential customers may question the quality and capabilities if what you're asking is a lot lower than what they were expecting to pay as a reasonable price for a truly superior solution.

CHALLENGE SECRET #5
The Big Idea Is a Big Deal

Over the years, I've had the privilege of helping thousands of students and a dozen or so high-profile consulting clients crush their challenges. One such student is Jackie from Austin, Texas.

I posted on social media that I was coming to Austin for a few days to do some work with Digital Marketer, and she and her husband reached out to my assistant and asked if they could pick me up from the airport and take me to my hotel. I said sure. After picking me up, they asked if I was hungry, to which I replied, "Of course; I'm always hungry!" So they took me to a very well-known BBQ spot called Blacks.

Jackie is no dummy. While we sat at a famous Austin barbecue joint, she asked me a bunch of questions about an upcoming challenge she was about to launch to grow her matchmaking business. I asked her the three questions I ask everyone before we start talking about challenges:

1. What are you selling on the back of your challenge?

2. What outcome does it promise, what problem(s) does it solve?

3. Who is the specific ideal customer for that offer?

Once she filled me in on those details, she showed me a list of potential challenge names she had brainstormed earlier with her husband, David.

As I was eating some of the best BBQ I've ever had in my life, I looked over the list of options, and with a mouth full of brisket and every finger drenched in BBQ sauce, I pointed to one of the three potential names and said, "that one."

"That's the one, that's the winner." Jackie was a bit taken aback by how quick and decisive I was about this. She asked me what I liked about that one and how I was so confident it would work. I later found out how right I was: That challenge generated thousands of happy customers, many happy marriages, and millions of dollars in revenue.

The reason I knew it was a winner is because it was a big idea. In fact, whenever someone tells me their challenge didn't do as well as they hoped, nine out of 10 times, it's because their challenge didn't have a big idea.

Let me explain what a big idea is and how you can come up with one.

The big idea should be the driving force behind the challenge. The hooks, the headlines, the stories, the daily training, and assignments all flow from the big idea.

Big ideas vary dramatically depending on who your customers are and what problem your offer solves, but here are some elements of what makes an idea big.

Below is The Big Idea Framework, which I created to help you brainstorm some potential big ideas.

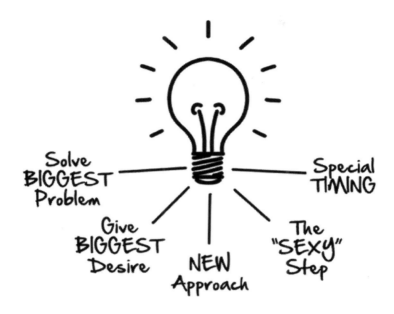

Again, after running over 75 live challenges for my own business, teaching, designing, coaching, hot seating, and consulting on more challenges than anyone else on the planet, I've boiled it down to these five places to look for a hot big idea:

1. **The Biggest Problem**: What is the biggest problem your customers know they have? If they already know they have this problem, designing a challenge that speaks directly to what's on their mind and what they believe is hindering them will immediately get and should be able to keep their attention.

2. **The Biggest Desire**: Does your ideal customer have a compelling big dream or desire? Above all, what do they want most? What do they really want? Most often, what our clients think they want is just the tip of the iceberg. Almost always there is a much deeper desire, a deeper what, and a deeper why in their heart and mind. Great marketers know what that is and create powerful language that grabs the attention and interest of your ideal customer.

3. **New Approach**: Let's face it, we like new. New triggers curiosity, and if you offer your customer a unique, fresh new approach, it will get your ideal customer leaning in wanting to learn more. No doubt that's a huge reason behind the success of my challenge model. It was a new approach to a big problem that made it possible for entrepreneurs to achieve their biggest desires.

4. **The Sexy Step**: After working with so many different people in different niches, I've seen my share of processes, frameworks, systems, and methods for how each of them creates results for their customers. One thing I've observed is that there is almost always a "sexy" step in the process. "What's a sexy step?" The sexy step is that one step or part of your process that all of your prospective customers obsess over. It's either the most fun, exciting part of your process—or it could be where they struggle the most—or maybe even it's the step in your process that people seem to lose their mind over when you teach or talk about it. When you design a Sexy Step Challenge, instead of covering your entire

process, you go deep into this one step, the sexy step, all five days.

5. **Special Timing**: There is a saying that timing is everything. While I don't know if I agree with that 100% of the time, it sure seems that timing is very, very, very important. Therefore, is there any special timing, big changes, or headlines in culture that are trending right now that you can use to create additional urgency and relevance for your challenge? Of course, just a few years ago, COVID-19 and the global shutdown created one of the most extreme examples of special timing the world has ever seen. But special timing could also be as simple as what time of year it is. Christmas, Easter, Thanksgiving, Black Friday, Summer, Back to School, New Year, Valentine's Day, and the list goes on of special timing opportunities that are available for designing a challenge big idea.

Here again is the big idea framework. If you or someone you know had a challenge flop, it's probably because they didn't have a big idea. And the most common reason they didn't have a big idea is because they don't have enough clarity on specifically who they are serving, the problem they are solving, and using messaging that is very easy to ignore. If you want additional free training from me on how to fix that, go to **www.ChallengeSecrets.com/BigIdea**.

CHALLENGE SECRET #6
Free Or Paid?
That Is the Question

There is a well-known saying in our industry that says, "Those who pay, pay attention." So, it makes sense that the question I get asked the most is:

"Pedro, should I run a free or paid Challenge?"

And the answer is you should probably be running both.

Each has advantages and disadvantages, so it's important to know when to use which for an optimal or at least a satisfactory outcome.

As we covered in Secret #1, I believe a free challenge is the most valuable lead magnet you can offer. Running free challenges is a phenomenal way to build your email list. I have built an email list of well over 300,000 people, and almost all of them signed up for one of my over 70+ free challenges.

The advantage of a free challenge is that it's much easier to get complete strangers to sign up for your challenge so they can hopefully fall in love with you and ultimately become a paying customer once you make your offer at the end of the challenge.

Free challenges also allow you to serve more people than in a paid challenge—which means more people will be exposed to you and hopefully be helped and impressed by you, which means ultimately more people will see and take your offer at the end of the challenge.

While size is the biggest advantage of free challenges, there are some negatives to running free challenges that you should be aware of as well. Sure, while it's much easier to get people to sign up for the free challenge, the next challenge becomes getting them to show up.

Sign Up Vs Show Up

Even with a well-designed free challenge, you will have about 10% of your free challenge participants (opt-ins) show up live on day one. It's also typical to see a 20% to 40% drop in live attendance from day one to day two.

In comparison, I recently ran a paid challenge where I had 394 of the 570 (70%) paid participants show up live on Day One and maintained those numbers all week long.

The other disadvantage to a free challenge is there are no barriers to entry. It's easier for spammers, scammers, and haters to join your challenge and create noise, unnecessary distractions, and chaos, making it more difficult for the others to participate.

Another disadvantage of the free challenge, especially very large free challenges like the ones people like Russell Brunson, Dean Graziosi, Tony Robbins, and I run, is that there are so many people it can feel somewhat impersonal and more difficult for participants to connect with you and each other.

CHALLENGE SECRET #6

This is one of the main benefits of paid challenges. All things being equal, paid challenges will almost always produce a smaller group of more committed people who will show up, be easier to support, and be 300% – 500% more likely to buy your offer since they have already proven their willingness to invest money for an outcome they want.

The Best of Both Worlds

After reading this, you may be wondering why anyone would want to run free challenges. And there are certainly days where I ask myself that same thing, but there's a reason some of the biggest entrepreneurs and businesses in our industry still run free challenges.

And the free challenges that we run are designed to be the best of both worlds. I call it a Freemium or Hybrid Challenge. This is a Free Challenge where anyone can join with a basic opt-in but offers the opportunity to upgrade to VIP. The free participants participate by watching the training in the free Facebook group, but the paid VIP participants get to join live on Zoom and interact with you and each other in ways not possible in the Facebook group.

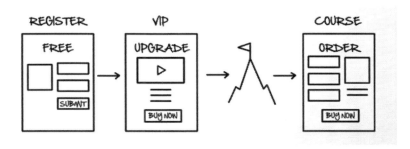

And since this is *Challenge Secrets: The Linchpin Edition,* I want to call special attention to the Freemium or Hybrid Challenge structure. Once you see how important this challenge structure is to the Linchpin's success, I may change the name from Freemium or Hybrid to a Linchpin Challenge.

This free challenge with VIP is the primary challenge structure being used right now by Russell and other entrepreneurs using Challenges as part of their Linchpin.

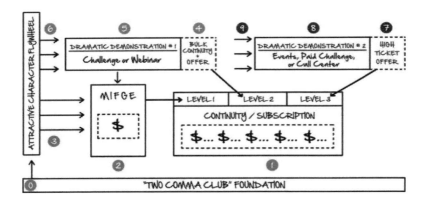

As you can see from the Linchpin Graphic, there is an arrow from the Challenge that points to the MIFGE, which then has an arrow that points to Level 1 of the Continuity / Subscription offer.

MIFGE stands for the Most Incredible Free Gift Ever. This concept has been around for decades and has proven to be quite effective. Classic examples of the MIFGE are the Columbia House Music Club and *Sports Illustrated* magazine.

CHALLENGE SECRET #6

Back in the day, Columbia House had this insane MIFGE. They would ship you eight CDs of your choice for a penny as long as you agreed to buy one a month at the regular club price. The regular club price was $19.99 per CD plus $8 shipping and handling, so all this was essentially a $29 per month music membership.

Each month you would get a catalog to pick what CD you wanted, and if you didn't respond in time, they would auto-ship you the month's selection.

At the peak around 1996, Columbia House and other similar clubs did approximately $1.5 Billion in revenue and represented 15% of the US music sales.

Sports Illustrated magazine also had a famous MIFGE. They offered to give you the Annual Swimsuit Edition and a football phone free for subscribing to the magazine.

CHALLENGE SECRETS

The models in this magazine were the absolutely most attractive and well-known at their time, and what sports enthusiast doesn't want a football phone?

The key to this strategy working is that these Most Incredible Free Gifts Ever (MIFGE) are not available for purchase anywhere. The only way to get the MIFGE is as a free bonus when you sign up for the subscription offer.

CHALLENGE SECRET #6

The MIFGE + Subscription offer works perfectly as the VIP upgrade offer in a Free Challenge.

When I came up with the idea of adding a VIP option to my free challenges, it was a $95 upgrade. This idea took off like crazy and is widely used in almost every free challenge I've ever seen.

I came up with the idea of the $95 VIP upgrade because I was now starting to increase my advertising spend. I remember the first time I spent $30,000, $50,000, and then $100,000 on Facebook ads per challenge.

Before the VIP upgrade, I used to keep my fingers crossed, having to wait five to seven days for the sales from the offer at the end of my challenge to repay my add spend and create a profit.

And while this always happened, it still made me a little nervous, especially as the ad spend kept increasing and eventually got to over $300,000 or more per challenge.

With the $95 VIP upgrade, I was now able to get reimbursed upfront for some, if not all, of my ads, which is often referred to as "liquidating" your ad spend.

And while many people still do this, if you want to implement the Linchpin, you're going to need to make a big shift here.

Instead of trying to liquidate some or all of your ad spend with the VIP, in the Linchpin, we use the VIP opportunity as a bonus along with other really cool bonuses for **FREE** when they sign up for your monthly membership or free trial of the subscription.

"Pedro, so you're saying I should give away the VIP upgrade and other valuable bonuses for FREE just for them agreeing to a FREE trial of my membership/subscription?" I'm not sure if you should, but that is exactly what Russell is doing in all of his Linchpin Challenges.

Russell is able to do this because he knows his numbers.

- He knows what percentage of people who sign up for a free trial will become a paying ClickFunnels customer.

- Once someone becomes a paying customer of ClickFunnels, Russell knows how long the average ClickFunnels customer stays a ClickFunnel customer.

- And most importantly, Russell knows how much money the average ClickFunnels customer is worth to the company, the Customer Lifetime Value (CLV).

Russell is so confident in his numbers and so focused on growing ClickFunnels' monthly recurring revenue that he is willing to take all the money that comes from the sale of the offers on the back of the challenges to cover the cost of ads.

Before Linchpin, we hoped to pay for ad spend with the VIP upgrade money and make our profit with the offer at the backend Challenge offer.

With the Linchpin, you're willing to use some if not all of the money from the backend offer to pay for the ads, so you can massively grow "the real business," your recurring revenue monthly membership/subscription.

CHALLENGE SECRET #7
The Perfect Challenge

"Pedro, I would totally run a challenge; I just have no idea what to teach each day."

I hear this all the time, so that's why in Secret #7, I'm going to show you one of my favorite ways for structuring challenge content as well as show you Russell's "Perfect" challenge content structure.

Before we talk about content, let's talk about the purpose of the challenge content and define the goal behind the daily training.

The image below is where things are before your challenge starts. Your potential customer is way over there on one side, and you and your offer are way over here on this side.

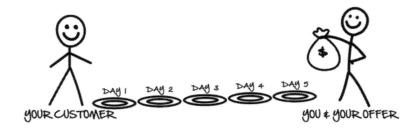

In a well-designed challenge, your challenger should be taking another step toward you and your offer each day of your challenge.

49

Before the challenge starts, it's very likely your challenge participant has no idea who you really are. But as each day unfolds, they are getting more and more value from you and are increasingly likely to choose to continue working with you.

In a well-designed challenge, where you've built trust with your participants, your challengers should be ready to work with you by day three, and some possibly made that decision even sooner.

By day five, your people, your right-fit customers as my friend Bari says, should be all in and ready for the next step. One of the things I love the most about my challenge method is that it doesn't require you to chase anyone. Instead, the people in your challenge take steps each day towards you and your offer.

Now that you understand what well-designed challenge content is supposed to do, here are two different ways to organize your content.

It's much easier to design a successful challenge when we are clear about the offer that you will be selling at the end of the challenge. This is why we covered foolproof offers in a prior secret.

The best question to ask yourself when thinking about the challenge content is: What are the most important objectives you want them to have over these five days that would best set them up for saying yes to you and your offer?

What are the most important things you want them to do and achieve?

What are the most important beliefs you want them to come away with?

What are the most important feelings you want them to feel?

The Step-By-Step Approach

I've noticed that the most successful, legitimate experts/coaches have one thing in common. They have a proven process, a framework, or some method they use to get results for their clients.

It often makes sense to structure a challenge around a process, too, with the goal of taking people deeper into your process one day at a time.

A simple example of this is a challenge I designed for my CPA friend Robert, who helps people find attractive mobile home park investments. We designed his challenge content around the process required to get a good deal on a mobile home park, and that's how the IEO Challenge was born.

To successfully acquire a good mobile home park deal, you first must:

1. **Identify** – Find a mobile home park that you're interested in that may or may not be currently offered for sale.

2. **Evaluate** – Gather and analyze the important facts so that you can determine the most amount of money you could pay for that property and still achieve your desired rate of return.

3. **Offer** – Make an offer to the seller at or below the price that you know will work for you, packaged and presented in a way that makes it attractive enough for them to say yes.

So let me show you how we structured this step-by-step challenge for my friend Robert…

Day 1: Day 1 is about the What and the Why behind the vehicle, which in Robert's case is mobile home park investing.

Day 1 in the IEO Challenge is a compelling look inside *what* Mobile Home Park investing is and why it's better than all other forms of real estate investing.

The goal of Day 1 is threefold:

1. Persuade them to see that your vehicle is the best.

2. Get them to commit to finishing the challenge.

3. Ensure they show up for Day 2.

I advise my students and consulting clients to approach Day 1 as if they were a trial lawyer going before a jury. Your job on Day 1 is to introduce the challenge participants to your vehicle and to persuade them to see for themselves why your way is *the* way.

If you do this well, the great majority of people who came to Day 1 will come back for Day 2. But if you don't do a great job on Day 1, then you can experience a large drop off in attendance and viewership between Day 1 and Day 2.

Even if you do a great job with Day 1 of a free challenge, it's not unusual to still see a 20-30% decrease in attendance. However, if your Day 1 content isn't very strong, you can see a decrease of 50% or more.

Day 2 of the IEO Challenge was all about Step 1 of the IEO Framework. I for Identify: where and how to potentially identify good mobile home park deals.

Day 3 would be on Step 2 of the IEO framework. E for evaluate. How to gather the necessary facts, figures, and financial data to know how much that mobile home park is worth, could be worth, and most importantly, what's the most you can offer while still achieving your desired rate of return.

Day 4 would be focused on Step 3 of the IEO framework, O for offer. This final step is all about how to put your offer together and present it to the owner.

Day 5 is a recap and shows the challengers the next step. The content agenda for Day 5 could be as simple as this:

1. Recap of the IEO framework process and what we learned this past week together.

2. Show more examples of deals Robert has done using the IEO framework.

3. Break down case studies of deals done by successful students/clients.

4. Invite them to his mobile home investing coaching program to get ongoing coaching and support from Robert so participants can get a great deal and avoid making a huge mistake on their first mobile home park investment.

By Day 5, the participants should be excited and ready to take that next step with you. All you need to do now is make them a foolproof offer that is focused on helping them get the desired outcome they want, which in this case is to get a great deal on their first mobile home park.

This is just one of several different ways to organize your challenge content. Please take the appropriate time to think through this step because if you get this wrong, there is a good chance your challenge will flop.

If you would like to speak with one of our challenge coaches about your challenge content design, go to our website for a free 15-minute challenge content coaching call:

ChallengeSecrets.com/Content

The "Perfect" Challenge

If you've been following Russell Brunson for any length of time, you've probably already heard of the Perfect Webinar. In the past, Russell and I had plenty of fun going back and forth debating which was better: the challenge or the webinar.

The truth is that both are powerful marketing methods that, when used wisely, can produce powerful results. However, even Russell has admitted that it's just so much simpler to learn how to crush a challenge first before trying to get a webinar to convert profitably.

And while Russell clearly now loves challenges, he still designs his challenges using the "Perfect" Webinar script when designing his day-by-day training.

Below is an image of Russell's "Perfect" Webinar script adapted for a 5-Day Challenge. This is literally a picture I took from his most recent *Linchpin* book.

CHALLENGE SECRETS

	MON	TUE	WED	THU	FRI
	Day #1	Day #2	Day #3	Day #4	Day #5
SPEAKER PRESENTATIONS (Total 40 min./day)	Origin + Opportunity + Vehicle False Belief	Internal False Belief	External False Belief	Stack + Close	Logic Repitch
GUEST SPEAKERS (Total 40 min./day)	2 Case Studies	2 Case Studies	2 Case Studies	1 Case Studies	1 Celebrity Speaker
CLOSING CTA (Total 10 min./day)	Get VIP FREE When You Upgrade And Get M.I.F.G.E.			Get Bulk Continuity + Offer	
VIP Q&A SESSION (Total 60 min./day)	✓	✓	✓	✓	✓
	Only For VIP Challengers Who Upgraded				

So let's look at how you could structure your challenge content using the power of the "perfect" challenge formula.

Day 1: Just like in my Step-By-Step framework, the vehicle is the star of the show on Day 1. Your opening origin story should not just be your origin story but your origin story as it relates to the vehicle.

Your goal is to have participants buy into the vehicle, fully persuaded just from the story alone. As you then get into more information about the vehicle, use facts, data, proof, examples, and more stories to eliminate any potential remaining doubt.

This also includes affirming what is true about the vehicle as well as identifying any lies and false beliefs they have about the vehicle and replacing them with truth.

> **PRO TIP:** When affirming the truth, you can build trust quickly with your audience by making them aware of what I call inconvenient or "negative" truths about your vehicle.

For example, on Day 1 of the Challenge Secrets MasterClass, I make it clear that running live challenges is a lot of work. This is the truth. However, what's also true is that I've never seen anything that's even remotely as effective at driving the results you want most. It's hard work, but it's worth it.

Day 2 in the "Perfect" Challenge is focused on helping your challenge participants get over their internal false beliefs about why their vehicle couldn't and won't work for them.

Again, you're going to want to think about the practical things that they are going to need to have and need to think to be able to say yes to your vehicle and your offer.

One of the things I've heard over the years from people is: "Pedro, I would totally do a challenge, but I'm not sure what to sell/I have nothing to sell."

This is a big internal issue, which is why on Day 2 of the Challenge Secrets Master Class, I go over all of the different types of offers you can make on the back of the challenge. And I make sure to put lots of focus on affiliate offers, which is the easiest and simplest of all the offers to make since it's not yours.

Day 3 in the "Perfect" Challenge is about the external limiting beliefs. These would be external factors that would prevent your challenge participant from being able to have success with your vehicle.

In the vehicle of running a successful challenge, it's usually traffic. "Pedro, I would totally buy your course and run a challenge, but I don't have an email list or a big social media following."

Therefore, on this day, we focus on the three main ways you can get people to sign up for your challenge:

1. Strategic Organic Social Media Posts

2. Referrals From Existing Challenge Participants

3. Affiliates / Dream 100

4. Paid Advertising

Day 4 in the "Perfect" Challenge is the day you open the cart. The day you tell people who are interested what the next step is. It's when you stack and close.

If you have already put together a webinar for this offer that converts or is used to convert, then this is when you use it.

To be clear, Day 4 or Day 5 is not about simply pitching and re-pitching your offer. A well-designed challenge should still be focused on delivering value and continuing to advance the participant further in the process of achieving the promised outcome of the challenge.

The people that will buy on Day 4 are more than likely your more emotional / impulse buyers. I love these people because I'm one of them. However, this is just a small subset of the market and of your sales, so it's important that we also help the logical buyers as well.

Therefore, Day 5 in the "Perfect" Challenge is about speaking more directly to the logical buyers, stacking, and re-pitching. Again, do not forget to bring at least one framework or one piece of valuable training, or many people will feel like Day 5 was a waste of their time.

In Russell's "Perfect" Webinar script, it says one Celebrity Speaker, which can be cool if you are able to do that, however, what I can tell you is powerful case studies and stories from your most successful students or past clients can be just as, if not even more, effective.

Choose a topic for Day 5 that ties everything together, remind them of where you have been day by day and step by step, and that your offer is just the next logical step if they want this result.

Day 5 is also usually a great day to have a guest speaker that can edify you, your vehicle, and your process. Ideally, this is someone who has personal results and experience with you and the vehicle.

Do not despise small beginnings. It's super cool that I now have become friends with some of the biggest entrepreneurs in our industry and, therefore, have gotten to work and consult on some of the biggest challenges online, but here is a tip for you.

> **PRO TIP: Do not underestimate the power of testimonials and case studies from "normal" people. One thing I am always continuing to look for and share are success stories from early-stage brand-new entrepreneurs who have made their first $1,000, first $10,000, and even their first $100,000 ever online.**

This is the longest secret in the book, and there's so much more I want to teach and share here, but we just don't have time.

If you want to get access to more of my Challenge Secrets so you can crush your very first or next challenge, go to **www.ChallengeSecrets.com/Course**.

CHALLENGE SECRET #8
Now Or Never

Now that you've been equipped with some of the most important Challenge Secrets, it's time to pick a date and commit to running your very first or next challenge.

You don't need to know the rest of the secrets in this book before you pick a date and commit. Look at your calendar and choose an upcoming Monday for Day 1 of your challenge. I'm going to give you three options. Ready?

Option 1: This coming Monday. Yes, that means this coming Monday. As you're about to learn, the only thing you need to run a challenge is an iPhone and a Facebook group. Running a challenge just 4 or 5 days from now is very realistic for you, no matter how little prep work you've done.

Option 2: Next Monday. Not this coming Monday but the Monday after that. This will give you a little more time to prepare and promote and will be the best option for most people.

Option 3: My least favorite of all the options is the following Monday, which is almost three weeks from now. The reason why this is my least favorite is because I've seen so many people pick a challenge date this far in advance that ultimately got scared, started overthinking everything, and ultimately chickened out and never did it.

So now it's time for you to pick a date and commit.

Remember: everything you want in your life and business is on the other side of you crushing it with challenges.

So it is time to pick a date, commit, and go over to **www.ChallengeSecrets.com/Commit** to let us know what date you selected, and I will send you a special free gift.

SECTION TWO
HOW TO RUN A LIVE
CHALLENGE

This is where the rubber hits the road. It's finally time to show up and serve your prospective customers by running your challenge…**LIVE**!

Yes, live. Really you. Really live, delivering value in real-time.

When I first introduced this idea to the marketing world in 2020, I got a ton of pushback from well-established experts and marketers. I got texts and DMs from a lot of big-shot marketers asking to learn more about what I was doing with these challenges.

After learning about my challenge model, almost every single one of them said the same thing. They all told me how much they hated doing stuff live.

One of them flat-out told me that he only does prerecorded stuff that can be immediately evergreened. And while I totally get the advantages of that, I made it very clear that's not what I do or how my system works. Funny enough, that marketer has run several live challenges, and at the time of my writing, is running ads for a 5-Day live challenge now.

One of the secrets behind the success of my challenge system is that it's live. Because it's live more people sign up, more people show up, and they show up with a different level of energy and excitement.

So now that you know how to design and promote your challenge, here are a few Challenge Secrets that will help you look like a pro when running your first or next live challenge.

Before going into those Challenge Secrets, let me address the potential elephant in the room because I don't want you to think I'm a hypocrite.

"Pedro, aren't you and Russell running The Challenge Secrets Masterclass as an evergreen challenge right now?"

Well, yes, we are. So clearly, at some point in your journey, it may make a ton of sense for you to consider running an evergreen challenge. _**BUT**_...not until you first learn how to crush it with live challenges.

If that's you and you're looking for the absolute best resource on how to crush it with an EVRGREEN challenge, go to **www.ChallengeSecrets.com/Evergreen** for more info.

CHALLENGE SECRET #9
The Pocket Challenge

There are a variety of different ways and formats for how you can run your very first or next challenge. To make this section of the book as helpful as possible, I am going to show you the simplest and most effective methods being used by me and my most successful students. This way, you can look like a pro, even if it's your very first time.

Let's get started with what I call a Level 1 Challenge.

How To Run A Level 1 Challenge

A level 1 challenge is a free challenge that requires nothing more than a smartphone and a Facebook Group.

This means you can absolutely run your very first or next challenge and quite possibly make your first $1,000, your first $10,000, and maybe even your first $100,000

- without a funnel or any landing page of any kind…

- without any paid ads…

- without any expensive cameras, lights, or microphones…

- and even without any fancy tech or computers.

To make money running a Level 1 Challenge, all you need is...

1. A smartphone

2. A Facebook group

3. A payment method

The payment method could be anything that allows people to send you money in a secure way. Most of the entrepreneurs I work with use platforms like Stripe, Paypal, Venmo, Cash App, and even Apple Pay. It really can be anything that is easy to use and secure.

So here's how you run a **Level 1 Challenge.**

Step 1: Create a Facebook Group

Create a Facebook group and name it after the name of your challenge so it's super clear that this group is for the people who are in your challenge.

This Facebook group is ground zero, command central, the whole enchilada...literally in a Level 1 Challenge, everything in your challenge happens in the Facebook group.

FACEBOOK GROUP PRO TIP #1*:* **Give your challenge Facebook group its own branded URL. This is done in the Facebook Group Settings under Group Settings / Customize Group / WebAddress.**

CHALLENGE SECRET #9

> **FACEBOOK GROUP PRO TIP #2:** Typically, these groups are private, which adds to the exclusivity of the challenge experience and prevents people from sharing content outside of the Facebook group.

However, sometimes I choose to make my Facebook group public so that I can get more visibility to the challenge and actually allow and encourage people in my challenge to share the daily trainings. Again, this makes sense if you want more visibility, don't mind having what you're teaching out in the public, and the nature of your challenge doesn't require your challengers to share personal information they may not want being shared outside of the group.

For more Facebook Group Pro Tips go to:

www.ChallengeSecrets.com/ProTips

Step 2: Go Live in Your New Challenge Facebook Group

"Pedro, why am I going live in this group if there is nobody in the group yet?"

It's crucial to post a live video before anyone even joins your group. The reason why is that it's the first video people will see once they come into your challenge group.

In this welcome video post, which you're going to make a pinned featured post in your group, you're going to do the following:

1. Introduce yourself.

2. Welcome members to the challenge.

3. Tell them what they are going to get out of the challenge and what's their payoff promised outcome/result for being here with you.

4. Tell them why you decided to run the challenge and give them important details such as the start date and time, how long each day, and when the challenge will end.

5. Give them their first homework assignment.

By doing this, the people in your challenge will have a short video to watch to confirm the good decision they made to join the challenge, what to expect, and what to do next.

This is a good time to ask them to do one or more of the following next steps:

1. Invite friends to join in the challenge.

2. Invite them to upgrade to the paid VIP experience.

3. Invite them to go live in the Facebook group to introduce themselves and what they are most looking forward to getting out of this challenge.

Step 3: Go Live on Facebook and Instagram

Now that you have created your Facebook group, you're ready to let people know about your challenge.

Hey friends…as some of you may know I [insert backstory—conflict/problem/struggle or desire].

Well, I finally…[tell them what happened, what you figured out, how you finally…].

So I decided to do a [insert name of challenge and details].

Tell them why you are doing it, who is it for, and to comment the word "Challenge"

So I decided to do a <<insert name of challenge and details>> tell them why you are doing it…Who is it for…and to comment the word "Challenge" if they want the link…and tag friends or anyone they know that might be interested in learning more about or getting this result.

Next, you simply monitor the comments of your lives as well as other posts and specifically look for all the people that commented "Challenge." Click on their name on the comment and shoot them a direct message saying hello and with a link to your Challenge Facebook Group.

Step 4: Go Live to Warm Up the Facebook Group

Go live in the group a day or two before the challenge starts to create and keep the excitement and momentum in your Facebook group.

You can share one of your core stories, or share a little about a concept you're going to break down further in the challenge, or you can maybe give a short overview of the challenge.

Step 5: Go Live on Day 1 Of Your Live Challenge

It's Day 1, so it's time to go live in your Facebook group with your training and assignment for Day 1.

And yes, you can do all this and go live right into the Facebook group on your iPhone. I would recommend a simple iPhone stand to hold your phone and keep it plugged into power while you're going live on Day 1 and each subsequent day.

How To Run A Level 2 Challenge

A level 2 challenge is a big step up from a level 1 challenge from a technology and complexity perspective. However, a level 2 challenge is not necessarily better than a level 1 challenge. The quality of any challenge comes from the quality of the big idea, the transformational training, and the assignments you deliver daily—not the level of complexity.

However, when you're ready to take your challenges to the next level, here is what a level 2 challenge looks like.

The 2-Page Free Challenge Funnel: Most, if not all, of the challenges you've participated in or seen advertised on social media had a challenge funnel.

The most basic free challenge funnel is a 2-page funnel where…

>Page 1 is The Challenge Registration Page.

>Page 2 is The Challenge Thank You Page.

For a free challenge template, go to **www.ChallengeSecrets.com/FreeFunnel.**

Now that we've covered the basic 2-page funnel, let's discuss the more commonly used 3-page challenge funnel.

The 3-Page Free Challenge Funnel: Here is the most typical way to create a 3-Page Challenge Funnel.

Page 1: This is the same Free Challenge Opt-in Registration page that's used in the 2-page funnel.

Page 2: Instead of being a thank you page, it's now used as a way to sell VIP / backstage pass offer. If it's a paid challenge, page 2 is usually some form of a Video Sales Page designed to sell the challenge.

Page 3: Thank you.

Reminder and Replay Emails: To get more people to engage with your training, either live or by replay, the effective use of emails is incredibly important.

Remember, one of the main reasons why challenges are different and typically outperform other marketing methods, such as lead magnets, webinars, or video sales letters, is because of how much value and results in advance they produce for your challenge participants before you ever ask them to buy something.

We always want to be thinking about how we can get more of our challenge participants to consume as much of the challenge training as possible.

Therefore, the best way to use emails in your challenge is to remind participants about an upcoming live session that's about to happen and then to email them with a link to the replay of the training that just happened.

IMPORTANT: Usually Day 4 of a 5-Day Challenge is when you officially invite participants into the next step of your offer.

Once the offer has been made on Day 4, you're going to want to make use of the PS section under your signature on the replay email on Day 4 as well as on the Reminder and replay emails on Day 5.

Challenge Hosting and Streaming: In a level 1 challenge, you go live from your phone directly into the Facebook group, but in a level 2 challenge, you have a couple of other options.

Zoom: You can live stream from Zoom right into your Facebook. What's cool about this is you can allow either your free and/or VIP challenge participants access to join the trainings live on Zoom while it's being streamed.

This has several cool advantages:

1. A Zoom meeting is a way more personal experience for your challenge participants, letting you get immediate feedback, take live shares, and easily do Q&A.

2. Some people prefer or need to watch the live trainings on Facebook, and by streaming it live from Zoom into the Facebook group, they can do that with no extra work for you.

3. The Facebook live in the Challenge Facebook group becomes an immediately available replay that can be pinned as a featured post in the group. This means there is no need to wait sometimes hours for the Zoom file to process, and no need to download or upload the file to a special replay area. It all happens automatically for free by Facebook. Thanks, Mark Z.

Paid Advertising: In the previous section, we talked about the different ways to promote your challenge and covered paid advertising there.

You can, of course, run a Level 2 and even a Level 3 challenge without paid advertising. You may remember me telling the story of my friend Richmond Dinh, who generated over $3 million in revenue before ever spending $1 on paid advertising.

At the time of this writing, specifically as it relates to Facebook and Instagram, it appears that platform changes are impacting the quality of the traffic myself and many of my friends, students, and consulting clients are experiencing.

So when you're ready to open up your wallet and invest serious money in advertising on Meta (Facebook and Instagram), it would be wise to start small and test to make sure that the views, clicks, and leads are the people you're actually looking for.

It also might make sense to work with a media buyer who actually knows what they are doing, which, unfortunately, is way more difficult than you would think. You may end up kissing a lot of frogs before you find a prince.

Serious Warning

I've seen many dreams die in the funnel and Facebook ads graveyard. By that I mean I've seen people postpone running a challenge while they learn how to build a funnel or learn how to run ads.

And then I never see them again. They seem to never re-emerge from that deep dive into all the details of what it takes to build a funnel or figure out Facebook Ad Manager.

So please do not make the mistake of putting off running a level 1 challenge now with the plans of learning how to build a funnel or run Facebook ads. If you don't already know how to do those things or already have the money to hire someone…forget about Level 2 for now and do yourself a huge favor and move forward planning and running a Level 1 challenge.

Now, I'll show you how to run a level 3 challenge.

How To Run A Level 3 Challenge

A level 3 challenge is essentially a level 2 challenge with one or more of these extras:

1. Text Notifications

2. Facebook Messenger / ManyChat Notifications

3. Streamyard / E-Camm

4. Daily Homework PDFs / Workbook

CHALLENGE SECRETS

In closing, please pick a challenge Level 1, 2, or 3 that you can do right now. Do not make this harder than it needs to be by burdening yourself with having to learn a bunch of tech while at the same time learning how to design and deliver a great live challenge.

CHALLENGE SECRET #10
Location, Location, Location

There is a classic real estate saying that says the three most important things in real estate are location, location, and location.

And just like in real estate, when it comes to running your challenge, you do have several options when it comes to location, so let's cover those here in Secret #10.

- The OG – A Private Facebook Group

- Zoom

- The Broadcast Challenge

The Private Facebook Group

This is where it all started and where it's likely to continue for the great majority of people running both free and paid challenges.

Running your challenge in a private Facebook group is just simple, easy, it's free, and the biggest advantage is that almost everyone you're trying to serve with your business already has the app on their phone and is already in the habit of going there multiple times a day, and more than likely even hourly.

Therefore, going live each day in your challenge Facebook group just makes sense. Why not put you and your challenge in a place they're already paying attention to? Additionally, Facebook has made it known that it is going to be giving preference to live posts, as well as posts from Facebook groups in the feed.

Why would Facebook do that? Think about it: Facebook wants to keep its users, get new users, and increase how much users are spending on the app. Therefore, Facebook is always thinking about how they can improve the user experience; therefore, the algorithm for what we all see in the Newsfeed is of utmost importance.

When a Facebook user requests to join a Facebook Group, that is a clear indication of interest. Therefore, Facebook is going to assume because you chose to join that group, that you would be interested in some of the "best" posts from that Facebook group in your feed.

One of the toughest things to get these days is organic reach with your Facebook, and running your challenges inside of a Facebook group is one of the best ways to get more people to see you in their feed.

The other advantage of running a challenge in the Facebook group is that it's going to create a flurry of activity. Views, comments, and posts are going to go up like crazy during challenge week. The algorithm is going to catch that and further prioritize that content in the feed, bringing even more attention to you and your challenge.

While many of us have a love/hate relationship with Facebook, the truth is I am very grateful for having the ability to use Facebook Groups for free as a place where I can run both my free and paid challenges to serve people all over the world while growing my business at the same time.

Zoom Meetings

We already covered in a prior secret how to use Zoom for your VIP Upgraded / Backstage Pass experience. However, Zoom can also be used as the main and even only place you deliver the challenge.

If you have a small challenge and you don't like the idea of only having a handful of people in the Facebook group, then you can choose to run the challenge entirely on Zoom.

This means if people want to attend live, they will need to be on Zoom. The advantage of this approach is that people will tend to prioritize the live training since it's on Zoom, which means you can expect a higher show-up rate. Additionally, I think it increases the level of vulnerability your challenge participants are willing to engage in since this is not "on Facebook."

> **PRO TIP:** If you run your challenge exclusively on Zoom, you will need to send out links or post the Zoom replays somewhere.

One of the advantages of running your challenge in the Facebook group is that once your Facebook live is over, that live training video gets processed and turned into a post that can be watched on replay essentially immediately.

Another cool feature of running your challenge on Zoom is the opportunity to do a Tiny Challenge™. "Pedro, what's a Tiny Challenge?" A Tiny Challenge is a cool name that my friend Richmond and I came up with for something he did when he first started running challenges.

When Richmond was first getting started as a coach, he only had a small handful of people signing up for his first few challenges. So, instead of going live in a Facebook group with only 3-4 people, he decided to offer a 1:1 challenge experience to each person that signed up.

Earlier this year, during the spring of 2023, Richmond flew into Orange County, California, so we could record a training together at my house. At one point during the training, he said, "When I first got started, I did like 13 or 14 one-on-one challenges."

I looked at him with a puzzled look on my face and asked, "You did what?"

And he said, "A 1:1 challenge."

Of course, I responded by asking, "What's a 1:1 challenge?"

I'm the challenge guy, and I've never heard of a 1:1 challenge. To this, Richmond laughed and then explained the simple concept.

A 1:1 challenge is essentially a live challenge that, instead of being run in a group for 1 to many, is a 1:1 coaching call you do with each challenger five days in a row.

If you have three people that sign up for your challenge, you will be doing three 1:1 calls each day for five days in a row. You're probably thinking, "Wow, Pedro, that sounds like a lot of work."

Well, if you're just starting out and you are in a time in your career where you could really use proof and your first few customers, you should 100% be willing to do this.

Richmond only did this a dozen or so times and has now gone on to generate millions of millions of dollars in his coaching business.

To learn more about Tiny Challenges, go to:

www.ChallengeSecrets.com/Tiny

The Broadcast Challenge

Now, if you don't want to deal with any of this Facebook or Zoom stuff, you can always just broadcast and livestream your challenge on your YouTube, Facebook Fan Page, Instagram, TikTok, and any other place like this.

People are still able to engage in the comments, but there is no other location or place where you are trying to gather them.

CHALLENGE SECRET #11
Want Some More?

One of the most difficult parts of a webinar, where almost everyone blows it, is transitioning from the teaching to the pitch. Even experienced successful entrepreneurs often end up fumbling their way through this. This is one of the biggest advantages challenges have over webinars.

A webinar is essentially a one- to three-hour sales pitch. They are very unforgiving. There are so many landmines that you can step on while doing a webinar. You could do almost everything perfectly, but if you step on even one of them, if you make just one of potentially dozens of mistakes, there goes all of your sales.

In a webinar, you get one shot to make your pitch and close the deal, and if you blow it…you blew it.

Challenges, on the other hand, are super forgiving.

A challenge is not a 5-day sales pitch or webinar. A challenge is not a sideways webinar. A well-designed challenge is a 5-day live training event where valuable, actionable training and daily action are taken.

The people having the most success with challenges are giving massive value for free or at a deep discount. Some of our best stuff is being delivered in our challenges as we are really helping people get into momentum and make real progress with whatever the challenge is about.

In a webinar, the best you can do is overcome sales objections with words and examples; in a challenge, you can actually help someone, not just overcome an objection. You can actually help them remove the obstacle standing in their way of getting the result they want.

That's The Big Difference...

Webinars overcome Sales Objections with words while Challenges help people overcome obstacles with work!

Given that a webinar is a one-time event, there isn't time to actually help the person achieve anything other than learning just enough about the opportunity and your offer to make a buying decision.

I've heard Russell say that when a webinar flops and fails to convert, nine out of ten times, it's because the person taught too much. In a webinar, teaching too much content makes it increasingly difficult to effectively transition to the pitch.

But with a challenge, you have five days to actually teach some of your best content and help your people make real progress every day, all while preparing them to take the next step with you once the challenge ends.

Which brings us to Secret #11. One of the coolest parts about using a challenge to sell your back-end offer is that you don't need to be a professionally trained salesperson or perfectly execute the perfect webinar to make sales.

CHALLENGE SECRET #10

If you've run a well-designed challenge, then by Day 4 and certainly by Day 5, the people in your challenge are ready to learn more about what's next, which, of course, is your fool-proof offer.

And because you've built know, like, and trust with them over the past five days, you really don't need some super slick presentation to sell your offer. Below is some language for how to easily transition from the challenge trainings into the offer.

"Haven't the last five days been great? We've covered [insert a key topic]…you accomplished [insert an outcome they completed]…and we even had you [insert another key achievement].

Look at how much progress you've made just in the past five days…imagine what we can accomplish together over the next [months/weeks] together.

Today can either be the end of the challenge or the beginning of us working together to ensure you achieve [insert outcome].

So, if you like what I've given you this week…would you like some more?

I want to credit my friend Bari Baumgardner for teaching me the line "Would you like some more?" It really is such a simple way to invite someone to continue going down the path with you.

CHALLENGE SECRET #12
Finish Strong by Following Up

The fortune is in the follow-up.
— Jim Rohn

There are two primary ways to sell your offer on the back of your challenge.

1. Send participants to a sales/order page.

2. Ask participants to book a call.

Typically, you will see offers of $2,997 or less be sold directly on a sales page, and offers of $4,997 and up are usually sold over the phone on a sales call.

Either way, only a small percentage of people (3- 5% of free challenges and 5-10% of paid challenges) will usually go to a sales page and purchase or book a call on their own.

And while this can be enough to have a profitable challenge, the fact is you can double and even triple the number of buyers and revenue with some simple follow-up.

Here is a simple idea you can use to follow up to increase the profitability and impact of your challenges: Challenge VIPs that have not yet purchased the back-end offer or booked a call.

Challenge VIPs that have not yet purchased the back-end offer or booked a call.

If you're running a free challenge that has a VIP option, start your follow-up efforts by focusing on the VIP buyers. VIPs have proven they are more interested in this experience by investing more time and money than free attendees.

The data also supports this. A VIP buyer is at least 5- 10 times more likely to purchase your offer than a free participant. In my experience, about 20% of your Challenge VIP buyers will purchase your back-end offer compared to about 2-5% of free challenge participants. Another interesting statistic is that approximately half of your buyers of your offer will come from VIPs. Again, these numbers can vary based on the price of your offers and other factors, but it's a good approximation of numbers I've seen over the years across many different businesses and niches.

Now that you understand the numbers, you see why it makes so much sense to follow up with your VIP buyers first.

I recommend reaching out to them with a personal message in either text, by phone, Facebook Messenger, or, in the worst case, email. The message should be as personal as possible, never automated. For example:

"Hi, [insert their first name], it was great having you in the challenge."

Then ask a question. Here are some examples:

What was your favorite part of the experience?

What was your biggest takeaway or breakthrough?

What part of the challenge did you think was the most valuable?

After they answer…you can respond with…

"That's great."

You can continue asking other questions in a conversational tone and nature but eventually, you want to ask them if they'd like additional help or support in achieving their desired outcome.

Once you're in the conversation and have a sense of what they want to accomplish, you can ask them directly about the offer.

"I'm curious, did you happen to see Pedro's invitation [insert name of offer]? Do you have any questions about it?

It seems like this could be a great help to you in achieving [insert result]. What do you think has kept you from joining so you can get the additional help you need?

These are just a few examples, some sample questions you and maybe your team can use to follow up with the people in your challenge who have not yet purchased.

With some simple question-based, no-pressure follow-up, you might be able to increase the number of clients and challenge revenue by as much as 25 – 50%, which I felt was a significant reason to follow Challenge Secret #12.

As I wrap up this section, I'm going to share with you maybe the most powerful forms of follow-up you can do after your challenge. And that is to run another challenge.

I can't tell you how many of my absolute best and favorite customers did not buy from me after attending their first challenge. I was shocked to find out that many purchased only after two and some even three challenges.

This is why, at some point, you're going to want to establish a rhythm, a challenge calendar of sorts. It could be once a month, every other month, or once a quarter, but regardless of the frequency, don't forget to invite past challengers to your future challenges.

CHALLENGE SECRET #13
Pick Up the Proof

In the game of sales, marketing, and persuasion, there is nothing more valuable than proof. In general, people want to avoid risk; nobody wants to make a mistake on purpose. The more proof you can provide about just how awesome your product or service is, the more likely and more quickly you are to get someone to buy from you.

The live training that you will deliver during your challenges will create an insane level of engagement. I just helped Bill, one of my most recent consulting clients, run his first challenge. Bill has successful multiple 7-figure businesses that he built on the back of webinars that, unfortunately, as of last year stopped being profitable.

On Day 1 of running his first challenge ever, Bill was hooked. I remember him calling me so excited about the over 700 people who showed up live and how engaged everyone was in the chat as well as in the Facebook group.

All this engagement created by the challenge not only leads to higher conversion rates of your offer but loads of social proof that you can repurpose and pretty much use everywhere.

This social proof can be used in promo, reminder, replay, and cart emails. They can also be used to create compelling hooks for emails and ads, as well as used on the challenge funnel and sales pages.

Here are the most common forms of social proof that you should collect along the way:

- Each day's training will be streamed live and available for replay in the Facebook group as a post. Comments made by your challengers on these video training posts will be insanely valuable to look at and screengrab.

- If you're running any part of your challenge on Zoom, the same will be true for the Zoom chat. You or someone on your team should review the Zoom chat to glean valuable feedback and powerful social proof.

- Homework posts and lives in the Facebook from challenge participants.

- Forms, surveys, and other processes you want to use to gather input in data in a more structured manner.

- Video testimonials using Boast.io or other platforms to collect video from people who had an amazing experience in your challenge.

Even if you're just starting out and have very "little proof," I think you will be pleasantly surprised with how much legit proof you can generate even with a relatively small challenge.

Given this is a special *Linchpin Edition* of *Challenge Secrets*, I wasn't able to cover all of the secrets to running an awesome challenge. If you would like more support to ensure you crush your first or next challenge, go to **ChallengeSecrets.com/Call** to book a free call with one of our Challenge coaches.

SECTION THREE
PROMOTING YOUR
CHALLENGE

In the movie *Field of Dreams*, Kevin Costner plays a character named Ray Kinsella, who is famous for saying something he never actually said.

You've probably heard the saying, "Build it, and they will come." Well, it turns out the quote is actually "If you build it, He will come," and Kevin Costner's character didn't say it; it's what he heard as he was walking through the cornfields.

In the movie, following this instruction led to a Field of Dreams. Unfortunately, the majority of entrepreneurs who take this as business advice end up disappointed.

In the first section, I shared the Challenge Secrets you need to know to design a great challenge that your ideal prospective customers are going to want to attend. So now that you've got an awesome challenge designed, it's time to get people to sign up.

In this section, I'll teach you how to promote your challenge so that you can get the right people to register for your free or paid challenge.

These Challenge Promotion Secrets are critically important to your success. Unfortunately, just being an awesome person and being great at what you do is no longer good enough.

When you diligently apply these Challenge Secrets, don't be surprised if you end up going from an unknown best-kept secret to the #1 go-to expert in your niche. So, if you're ready to learn how to fill up your challenges with the right people, here's Challenge Secret #14.

CHALLENGE SECRET #14
Fill Up Your Challenge for Free

Social media has profoundly changed how we do life and business. Before the explosion of social media, businesses had to rely upon traditional media like TV commercials, radio spots, magazine and newspaper placements, and direct mail to find new customers and grow their business. While there are still billions of dollars of advertising still happening on these traditional platforms, social media has made it possible for anyone to draw attention to their business for free.

When I ran my first-ever challenge back in May of 2018, I invested about $3,000 in Facebook ads and got approximately 300 of my ideal customers to sign up. I will be sharing some of my paid ad secrets later in this section.

And while paid advertising has been very good to me, I know that many of my past students either didn't have the money and/or didn't know how to run paid ads when they were first getting started. So here is Challenge Secret #14 to the rescue.

I'm going to share with you a super simple yet incredibly effective way to get people into your challenges for free with organic traffic. I will focus on Facebook, but this same strategy can be applied on Instagram, LinkedIn, TikTok, and YouTube.

Of all my students, I believe Richmond most impressively harnessed the power of free organic traffic for launching and growing his business with challenges. Richmond ran 30 challenges and got to well over $3 million in sales before ever spending $1 on paid advertising. Below are the exact steps for how to generate challenge sign-ups for free using social media.

Step #1 – Post: Make a post on Facebook that gets people to leave a comment. Below are examples of the various types of posts. Again, the goal of these posts is to get people to self-select by leaving a comment.

Step #2 – Connect: Once they leave a comment on your post, it's time to start a conversation. Send a direct message to that person thanking them for leaving a comment on your post. Now you can learn more about what they are up to and see if they might be a good fit for what you do. You should never assume that they are or are not.

Step #3 – Invite: Invite interested people to your free Facebook group. This is the same free Facebook where you will be hosting your free challenge.

I know what you may be thinking. "Pedro, this seems like it would take a long time to get any momentum like this." It seems that way. But in reality, this is a powerful, proven way to make your first $1,000, $10,000, $100,000, and for some, potentially even your first $1 million online before you ever have to wander into the treacherous waters of paid advertising.

Richmond used this exact same method to do his first 30 challenges and generate over $3 million in revenue before ever running paid ads. So if you are just getting started, what if it was possible to make your very first $1,000 online, even have your first $10,000 per month or more with just 30 minutes of focused effort a day?

If that were possible, would you commit to doing it? Well, it is possible. Richmond and many other people have successfully used this strategy to go from $0 to $10,000 / month and even as much as $30,000 per month with the 30 / 30 / 30 Method, all with just making three posts per week. That's right, three posts a week, so here is the simple 30 / 30 / 30 framework based on the three simple steps we shared earlier.

Step 1 – Post: Make three posts per week: one on Monday, one on Wednesday, and one on Friday.

Step 2 – Connect: Spend 30 minutes per day connecting with people in Messenger. You will spend approximately 10 minutes connecting with each person, so you should be able to easily connect with at least three people in those 30 minutes.

Step 3 – Invite: Invite each of the three people you connected with in Messenger to your Free Facebook. If you invite three people into your group 1 in 3 should say yes and end up in your free group and get to experience your challenge.

So here is the breakdown:

- 30 minutes a day

- 30 days in a row

- Will get 30 people into your free challenge

- With 30 people in your free challenge, if you apply the Challenge Secrets, you should generate $10,000, $20,000, and as much as $30,000 a month or more in sales

CHALLENGE SECRETS

That's why it's called the 30 / 30 / 30 Method. If you've been looking for a simple no-money out-of-pocket way to get people into your challenge, here it is.

CHALLENGE SECRET #14

I'm Looking To Work With a Small Handful of Coaches, For Free, For 10-Days, To Help Them Get Clients Before Christmas . No Catch. Just Give Me a Review If You Got Value. Who Wants More Details? 🙋‍♂️🙋‍♀️

119   169 comments • 5 shares

It's Official! I'm Launching a 5-Day Course Creation Challenge To Help Coaches Create, Build & Launch Their Course In Less Than 5-Days! Who Wants More Deets? 🙋‍♂️
🙋‍♀️

106   135 comments • 1 share

How To Grow Your Challenge by 25% Or More Easily for Free

"But Pedro, what about paid ads?"

Yes, of course, at some point, running paid ads will more than likely make sense. However, at the time of writing this book, it appears to me that many online marketers, even many of the well-known "gurus" are struggling a bit when it comes to profitably running paid ads.

Therefore, unless you already have experience with paid advertising, I would encourage you to focus on the organic marketing and affiliate opportunities I discuss in this book when getting started.

> **DISCLAIMER:** There are exceptions. When I launched back in May of 2018, I launched by running ads directly to cold traffic and was able to have massive success right away, even though nobody knew who I was.

"Well, Pedro, can I do that?" Yes and no.

The answer is no if you are doing what everyone else is doing and saying what everyone else is saying. If that's the case, there's no chance you're going to have success with paid traffic, especially when you're just getting started.

However, the answer is yes if you are willing to follow my proven playbook for becoming a disruptive 1 of 1 force so who you are, what you say, and how you do what you do cuts through this noisy market like a hot knife through butter. I've done this four times in my own businesses and helped my most successful students and consulting clients do this exact same thing.

To learn more about this unconventional but incredibly effective playbook, I made you a short free training at

www.ChallengeSecrets.com/1of1

CHALLENGE SECRET #15
Who Else Has Your Ideal Customers?

Hopefully, by now you're seeing a clear path to filling up your very first or next challenge with free organic traffic or paid ads. Depending on your experience and the size of your team, you can certainly do both.

However, from my experience, I recommend getting really good at one traffic source and then adding a second one later. So before I ask you to decide which is going to be your primary traffic strategy for filling up your first or next challenge, let me share this third and final option.

To finish off this section on how to fill up your challenge, I want to share one last challenge traffic secret that has personally added millions of dollars to my business over the years and has also allowed me to meet some of my absolute favorite customers.

This process is a brainstorm/research exercise where you are going to write out a list of influencers, websites, or companies that already have gathered your ideal customers.

Here are some ideas to get your juices flowing. I promise that when you take just a few minutes to start this process, you will begin to see that the people you want and need to launch and grow your business are seemingly everywhere and easily within your reach.

The 10 X 5 Concept

1. Who are your top ten customers/clients?

   Who else do they know that could benefit from what you've done for them? People tend to hang out with and be friends with people like them.

2. What are the top 10 Facebook Groups where your who is already in?

3. Who are the top 10 influencers they are following on Facebook / Instagram?

4. What are the top 10 YouTube Channels your who is subscribed to and watching regularly?

5. What are the top 10 podcasts they are regularly listening to?

One great place to look when doing your research as part of this exercise is to not just look for people and places where your ideal customer is already gathering but also to go one level up and look for the people who have already gathered your niche market and potentially even your sub-market.

For example, as "The Challenge Guy," I am the #1 Go-To Marketing Industry Expert on Challenges. That is my micro-niche. Therefore, a great place for me to look for people who already have my ideal customers is to go up one level to the niche-market.

As "The Challenge Guy" in my micro-niche of Challenge Funnels, the broader upmarket niche market from Challenge Funnels would be Funnels. And, of course, the king of that niche is Russell Brunson.

Russell and I have been working together for the past couple of years, and it's been a win-win-win.

It's been a win for Russell because the more ClickFunnels trials or paying users that successfully build Challenge Funnels, the more likely they are to continue using ClickFunnels. Additionally, Russell got access to my best-in-class challenge training, as well as a new hook promoting the Challenge Secrets Masterclass evergreen challenge as a Linchpin Challenge for creating new ClickFunnels trials.

Of course, it's a win for me to get exposure to a larger audience in the bigger niche market of Funnels that may want additional challenge training or consulting from me.

And it's been a win for our mutual customers who benefit from getting access to training from two experts, not just one.

When pursuing affiliate or joint venture relationships with other entrepreneurs, look for how you can create a win-win-win outcome.

First, start with your mutual customer in mind. How do they win from this potential relationship? How does this benefit and add value to them? This should come first. I see many affiliate/JV relationships that don't seem to be an obvious win for the customer.

After putting the customer first, I believe you should next prioritize your prospective JV partner. Have an honest dialogue about what they want out of this relationship. Be sure to find out what would really make this a win for them.

Now that you believe this is truly a win for your mutual customer and know what your partner needs to win, it's time to be honest with them about what would make this a win for you.

Joint Venture and committed affiliate relationships can be an absolute game changer for launching and growing your business. I hope the advice provided here in Challenge Secret #15 will help you create high-quality, profitable relationships.

I'm always looking to create more win-win-win relationships, so if you have an interest in learning more about how we could work together, go to **www.ChallengeSecrets.com/partner.**

FREE GIFT

I am so excited for what is going to be possible for you now that you have decided to apply these little-known Challenge Secrets. While more and more entrepreneurs are becoming aware and even using Challenges, it's very clear to me that they are doing so unaware of my Challenge Secrets covered in this book.

This book contains the exact process and Challenge Secrets I've used to take my career from a bored financial planner living in obscurity to a leading marketing expert with a business that does over $10 Million a year in sales. These Challenge Secrets have transformed my life, gotten me invited to speak on dream stages, and connected me to some of the biggest entrepreneurs and thought leaders in the world.

To help you make the most of this book, I want to start by giving you a free gift that will all but guarantee you crush your first challenge.

My 8-Figure Challenge Secrets Worksheet will literally walk you through my proprietary process that took me from $0 in online sales to over $10,000,000 in sales in just my second year.

Normally, you'd have to invest upwards of $1,000 or more to get access to it, but for a limited time, you can get it absolutely free right now at **ChallengeSecrets.com/FreeGift.**

CAN I CHALLENGE YOU?

I have rarely talked about this publicly, but as a child and even into my teenage years, there were many, many nights I would cry myself to sleep. Fortunately, I wasn't being bullied at school or being tormented by nightmares. But I would lie in bed, and while trying to fall asleep, I couldn't help but start thinking about dying.

I don't know why and don't even remember when this started exactly. But way more nights than not, I would lay in bed and just start crying at the thought of my death.

At some point, it started happening less and eventually went away altogether. At the time, I really had no idea what was going on. I was a happy kid, had a great childhood, awesome family, and really had no idea why I was so preoccupied with dying.

Little did I know it would take almost 25 years before I discovered what that was all about. Turns out I wasn't afraid of dying. I was actually terrified of living a life that didn't matter.

Long before I had the tools or the direction, deep down, I had a desire to do something significant with my life. I have a feeling if you've made it this far in this book, that's probably true for you as well.

I believe that desire that you and I both have is the desire to be great. Webster defines great as of ability, quality, or eminence considerably above the normal or average.

Again, if you've made it this far in this book, I know you have a desire to be great because you are certainly not normal or average. Normal and average people don't buy books like this, let alone finish them.

Can I tell you, there is nothing wrong with wanting to be great. I believe there is something wrong with NOT wanting to be great.

Have you ever desired greatness? Usually, as kids growing up, we dream about being sports heroes, astronauts, famous singers, or maybe even a movie star.

Twenty-five years later, in May of 2018, I ran my first free challenge, The 100X Academy Masterclass. Little did I know that my whole life was about to be flipped upside down in the best way possible. At the time, I was 43 years old. I was a financial professional doing very well, with plans of expanding my financial business, but God had other plans.

In that first challenge, something shifted. I came alive in a way I had not experienced before. It's as if everything in my life before had perfectly prepared me for this new life. A life I was only able to discover after running my first challenge.

One of my mentors says, "When you find your people, you find your purpose."

Within a few months of running my first challenge, I ran several more. For a few months, I was running a challenge twice a month.

I couldn't help myself. I couldn't believe it was possible to have this much fun, changing people's lives, and getting paid to do so. And when you find your people, you really do find your purpose.

And when you find your purpose, you'll discover what you were born to do.

It was in the Summer / Fall of 2018 with 100X that for the first time in my life, I could visibly see that I was having a significant impact on people's lives. I mean, serious life-changing transformations were happening for hundreds of people from all over the world in just the first few months of something God tricked me into starting.

> ***The greatest tragedy in life is not death but life without a purpose.***
>
> ***– Myles Munroe***

In 2018, I was 43 years old, and for the first time in my life, I was doing something that I knew mattered. I mean, it really mattered. I wish I could explain to you the fulfillment that comes from seeing something you created changing people's lives for real in a very meaningful way.

All the problems, pain, and past mistakes of my life now made sense. All the things I had learned over the years being involved with so many different companies and even industries were now coming together.

> **Help enough people with their problems, and yours will go away. Service to many leads to greatness.**
> **– Jim Rohn**

> **If you help enough people get what they want, you can have everything you want.**
> **– Zig Ziglar**

As we get to the end of this book, I hope and pray this is not the end, but instead the beginning.

The beginning of the rest of your life, being the best of your life, all because of one decision. One decision I hope you've already made. The decision to run your first or next challenge as soon as humanly possible.

I can't even begin and frankly don't even want to try and imagine what my life would look like today had I never committed to Crushing It With Challenges.

Pretty sure I could say the same thing for many of my friends and students people like Stephen and Chelsea, Tresa Todd, Russell Brunson, Sean Cannell, Dean Graziosi, and so many more.

Many of our stories have been shared throughout the book to give you real-life examples to help you better understand the

Challenge Secrets. But there is another reason I shared so many of our challenge success stories for you to see it's possible. And not just possible, but possible and probable for you.

In addition to writing you a book with the absolute best information on challenge marketing, I was equally as committed to doing so in a manner that would give you the hope and belief you need to actually do it.

You see, knowing these Challenge Secrets isn't enough. I feel compelled to remind you that I, my friends, and the many students of mine who have seen staggering life-changing results were only possible because we **APPLIED** these Challenge Secrets.

Remember Challenge Secret #1 - You're Just One Challenge Funnel Away. This is true, but maybe for a reason you don't see it yet. You see, I don't think I have ever met anyone who ran their first challenge and didn't get bit by the "Challenge Bug." I wish I had a better name for it, but I don't. The Challenge Bug is a term I use for what happened to me, Sean Cannell, John Acuff, Roland Frasier, and Dean Graziosi…and that is after running our first challenge, we all left feeling and saying the same thing: "That was awesome…I'm for sure doing that again."

Now you may be thinking, "Pedro, these people made multiple six and even seven figures on their very first challenge. Of course they couldn't wait to do it again, but what about us regular people?"

The same hold true. I can't tell you how many times I've talked to people who ran their very first challenge and didn't make much or any money at all, and they too left drawing the same conclusion. That challenges are awesome and they are for sure doing another one.

As I wrap up this book, here is my invitation to you. Earlier in the book, I asked you to commit to a date for when you're going to run your first challenge. If you happened to read through that part without committing to a date, now is the time to commit.

Don't let these Challenge Secrets exist as just ideas on the page when they can be used to change your life and shape your destiny.

Here's to you Crushing It With Challenges.

Your Friend,

Pedro "The Challenge Guy" Adao

ABOUT THE AUTHOR

Pedro Adao went from a completely unknown industry outsider to now widely recognized as a marketing industry-leading expert...

From $0 sales online to well over $10,000,000 a year in revenue in just his second full year...

From being a financial planner living in obscurity in 2018 to now leading the 100X Movement, the #1 Training Program and Community for Kingdom Entrepreneurs and becoming the #1 go-to Marketing Industry Expert on Challenge Marketing.

Pedro Adao is a father, husband, 10-Time ClickFunnels Two-Comma Club Award Winner, and recipient of the Two-Comma Club C $25 Million Dollar Award. He was also a speaker at one of the largest marketing events in the world, Funnel Hacking Live (FHL) in 2021.

Pedro is a highly sought out speaker & consultant. If you would like to have Pedro Adao speak at your next event, or if you would like to have him consult on your challenge or business, visit his website:

PedroAdao.com